Recqt DS

D0261345

THE WEST INDIANS
HOW THEY LIVE AND WORK

Uniform with this book

The Argentines: How They Live and Work
by Dereck H. N. Foster

The Australians: How They Live and Work
by Nancy Learmonth

The Austrians: How They Live and Work
by Eric Whelpton

The Brazilians: How They Live and Work
by R. A. Wellington

The Chinese: How They Live and Work
by T. R. Tregear

The Dutch: How They Live and Work
by Ann Hoffmann

The Finns and The Lapps: How They Live and Work
by John L. Irwin

The French: How They Live and Work
by Joseph T. Carroll

The Greeks: How They Live and Work
by Brian Dicks

The Irish: How They Live and Work
by Martin Wallace

The Italians: How They Live and Work
by Andrew Bryant

The Japanese: How They Live and Work
by W. Scott Moreton

The Russians: How They Live and Work
by W. H. Parker

The Spaniards: How They Live and Work
by Michael Perceval

The Swedes: How They Live and Work
by Paul Britten Austin

The United States: How They Live and Work
by David and Margaret Smith

The West Germans: How They Live and Work
by Reginald Peck

The West Indians
HOW THEY LIVE AND WORK

❧

Basil E. Cracknell

DAVID & CHARLES

NEWTON ABBOT   LONDON   VANCOUVER

To Sylvia

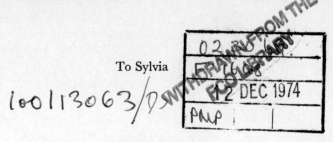

0 7153 6671 8

Set in 11 on 13pt Baskerville
and printed in Great Britain
by Devonshire Press Ltd Torquay
for David & Charles (Holdings) Limited
South Devon House Newton Abbot Devon

Published in Canada by Douglas David &
Charles Limited 3645 McKechnie Drive
West Vancouver BC

Contents

List of Illustrations

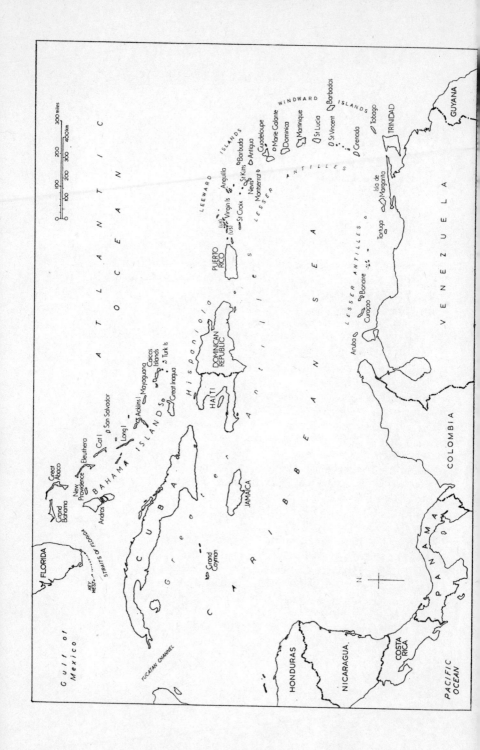

Foreword

THERE ARE 17½ million people living in the West Indies (excluding Cuba) and they are fortunate enough to inhabit one of the most beautiful regions of the world—perhaps the world's greatest natural playground. A region of warmth and sunshine, coral strands, waving palms, blue waters and, in places, dense unexplored jungle—to all of which the tourist brochures frequently do even less than justice.

Yet this natural paradise has been the scene of some terrible events in history: slavery, endless wars, the ravages of disease and, until recently at least, grinding poverty. Occasionally the region has experienced some of the world's worst natural disasters with hurricanes, earthquakes and volcanic eruptions.

Out of this strange amalgam of natural beauty and man's inhumanity to man has emerged a new society, perhaps the world's most recent ethnic group (so recent that some authorities do not yet accept that it even exists)—the West Indians. Nowhere in the world is there a more polyglot society of people speaking so many different languages and representing so many different cultures and traditions. It is this strange mixture of African, European, American and Asian religions, language, music, art and manners, that gives to the West Indian scene its colour and drama.

The true West Indian is an islander. Whereas the Guyanese and Belizeans look as much to their continental hinterlands as to the islands, the West Indians see only the sea whichever way they turn. While retaining the insularity of the islander, they are at the same time outward-looking.

9

And because each island is so different (some are semi-arid, almost desert islands, like the Turks and Caicos Islands, whilst others, like Dominica, have dense rain-forests), the West Indians have a remarkable individuality of character to match their insularity. It is precisely this individuality, of the islands themselves as well as of their inhabitants, that presents a great problem to any writer. Generalisations are unavoidable in a short book, but they are not without pitfalls.

Even a generation ago this book could hardly have been written: it would have seemed nonsense to imply that there was a recognisable community of peoples called the 'West Indians'. But so rapid and profound have been the changes which have taken place in the region since the war that this is no longer the case. Every year sees the region drawing closer together into a vaguely defined, yet very real, West Indian consciousness. For all their individuality the West Indians are fast becoming a people who feel a deep affinity with one another, and whose way of life and work is taking on a unity. This indeed is the basic rationale of this book.

I

The Region and the People

A geographical expression?

Do THE West Indies constitute more than a 'geographical expression' (Metternich's description of Italy in 1849)? Is there a recognisable and genuine West Indian identity or are the West Indians, to quote one of their poets, simply 'mimic men'? One writer, Getzel Pearcy, has stated flatly that 'no common culture of note has evolved other than that dictated by economic necessity'. But another experienced writer on the West Indies, Graham Norton, has described it as 'a formed society that has displayed unique characteristics for a very considerable period of time'. The debate goes on, and will probably go on indefinitely. But one indisputable fact is that the West Indians are becoming less and less insular in outlook as time goes by: they travel more, read more, and take an ever increasing interest in the region of which they are a part. And as they do so they come to realise that they have closer affinities with other West Indians than they have with people elsewhere. A genuine West Indian consciousness is being formed and it will develop and grow in the years ahead. As Sir Arthur Lewis told the students of the University of the West Indies in his graduation address in 1971: 'We strive to be ourselves, not Englishmen, or Africans, or Indians, or Chinese, but West Indians.'

The term 'the West Indies' is normally taken to refer to

THE WEST INDIES

Country	Size (sq miles)	Population (latest est) (000)	Principal languages
British Commonwealth and Dependencies			
Jamaica	4,411	1,960	English
Trinidad and Tobago	1,980	1,040	Eng Hindi Patois
Barbados	166	254	English
Bahamas	5,386	168	English
Dominica	289	74	Patois Eng
St Lucia	238	110	Patois Eng
St Vincent	150	95	Patois Eng
Grenada	133	105	Patois Eng
Antigua	170	65	English
St Kitts/Nevis	101	29	English
Anguilla	35	6	English
Montserrat	39	15	English
Turks and Caicos	166	6	English
British Virgin Islands	59	11	English
Cayman Islands	100	11	English
TOTAL	(13,423)	(3,949)	
French Antilles			
Martinique	425	425	French
Guadeloupe	680	334	French
Netherlands Antilles			
Curaçao	179	149	Dutch Papiamento
Aruba	71	61	Spanish
Bonaire	112	8	English
Dutch Leeward Islands	33	12	Dut Fr Eng
Others			
American Virgin Islands	132	63	English
Puerto Rico	3,423	2,754	Span Eng
Dominican Republic	14,722	4,325	Span Eng Patois
Haiti	8,500	5,400	Patois Fr
GRAND TOTAL	41,700	17,480	

Capital city	Currency	Political status
Kingston	J $	Independent member of British Commonwealth
Port of Spain	T/T $	,,
Bridgetown	EC $	,,
Nassau	B $	,,
Roseau	EC $	Associated state in British Commonwealth
Castries	EC $	,,
Kingstown	EC $	,,
St George's	EC $	Independent member of British Commonwealth
St Johns		Associated state in British Commonwealth
Basseterre	EC $	,,
Sandy Ground	EC $	British dependency
Plymouth	EC $	,,
Grand Turk	J $	,,
Roadtown	US $	,,
Georgetown	CI $	,,
Fort de France	Franc	Overseas department of France
Basseterre	Franc	,,
Willemstad	Neth/Ant	Integral part of Netherlands
Oranjestad	Florin	,,
Kralendijk		,,
Charlotte Amalie	US $	Unincorporated territory of the USA
San Juan	US $	Commonwealth in association with the USA
Santo Domingo	Gold peso	Independent
Port au Prince	Gourde	Independent

the islands of the Caribbean that stretch from the Cayman Islands in the west to Barbados in the east. Strictly speaking, Cuba should be included, but it is so much larger than the other islands (it is almost as large as all the others put together) that it is often considered as a separate entity and this book follows that practice. On the other hand, whereas again strictly speaking the Bahamas should be excluded, because they lie outside the area bordering the Caribbean Sea, they are in every respect so typical of the West Indies that it seems more sensible to include them. Bermuda, however, lies so far out in the Atlantic ocean that it is invariably excluded. This then defines the term 'the West Indies' as used in this book.

The archipelago of the West Indies extends over an area the size of the Mediterranean. As the table shows, the islands vary greatly in size and population. While some of the islands are within sight of the next ones in the chain, others are separated by 100 miles or more of sea—Jamaica, in particular, is about 125 miles from the nearest island. 'Insularity', it has been said, 'is a basic fact of West Indian life.'

Volcanoes, earthquakes and hurricanes

Geologically the West Indian islands represent the tops of submerged mountain chains: sometimes just the mere tip of the mountain projects above water, but elsewhere they rise to over 10,000ft as in the island of Hispaniola. Dominica, an island about twice the size of the Isle of Wight, has mountains rising to almost 5,000ft. Many of these mountains are volcanoes and a few are still active, such as Soufrière on St Vincent which showed such ominous signs of activity in 1972 that 1,500 people nearby had to be temporarily evacuated. Such a disaster as that of the complete destruction of the city of St Pierre, Martinique in 1902, when Mont Pelée erupted suddenly and 28,000 people lost their lives in a holocaust of fire, is still just within living memory . . . no one treats volcanoes lightly in the West Indies.

Earthquakes are another natural hazard that the West Indians have had to live with. Kingston, Jamaica has been hit by earthquakes or tremors several times: the ruins of the old Port Royal, which was completely destroyed by an earthquake in 1692, are now being excavated. As recently as 1907 Kingston was again destroyed by an earthquake followed by a tidal wave and 800 people lost their lives.

But the most serious natural hazards of all are the hurricanes. Ever since Christopher Columbus rode out his first hurricane off Santo Domingo, the West Indies has been renowned for its hurricanes. Autumn is the hurricane season, particularly the months of August to October. On average about five or six hurricanes hit the West Indies each year (but not all of these are of disaster proportions), when winds of up to 130mph have been recorded. The hurricanes are hatched out in the Atlantic and cross the West Indies from east to west, usually veering northwards towards the Gulf of Texas. Only Trinidad and Tobago seem to be safe from them. Fortunately, the onset and direction of hurricanes can be forecast fairly accurately now, thanks to the work of the National Hurricane Centre, Miami and sufficient warning is given for people to take shelter, although casualties can still be heavy: Hurricane Flora for instance killed 4,000 people in Haiti in 1963 and rendered 100,000 homeless. The damage to growing crops, particularly the banana plants, can often be serious, while the torrential rainstorms which frequently occur in association with the hurricanes do great damage to roads and bridges. The risk of hurricanes is an ever present feature of West Indian life. It affects the design of buildings, the location of towns and villages, the breeding programmes for new varieties of crops, the choice of building materials and the very attitude of the West Indians to Nature itself.

Benign climate

If it were not for the hurricanes, the climate of the West

Indies could probably be described as the most benign in the world. In fact one of the local languages of the Caribbean, Papiamento, spoken in Curaçao, has no word at all for weather! The temperature hardly varies during the year within the range 75–85° F (24–29° C), the skies are nearly always blue, the sun is nearly always shining and when rain comes (which is quite often), it tends to come in short sharp showers. There is often a welcome breeze, the balmy southeast trades which are sometimes called 'the Doctor', as opposed to the cool winds blowing off the land which they call 'the Undertaker' in Jamaica.

It never freezes in the Caribbean and snow is virtually unknown. If there are extremes of climate it is sometimes of rainfall. In Dominica for instance up to 400in of rain per annum has been recorded in the highest parts of the interior, which makes this one of the wettest places on earth. Yet on neighbouring Antigua the rainfall is so low that there has been until recently an acute shortage of water. Location with respect to mountains can make a great difference. In the Blue Mountains of Jamaica the rainfall can exceed 200in per annum, whereas at Kingston, only 15 miles away, the average rainfall is only 29in per annum. Cacti are frequently found in the semi-arid rain-shadow areas of the West Indies. In fact drought has been in recent years as serious a problem for agriculture as are hurricanes, and irrigation has become necessary on many of the islands. Moreover, unendingly warm and sunny days can become rather monotonous; at least a spell of rain gives people something to talk about. When Lady Nugent arrived in Jamaica in 1800, she remarked to Lord Balcarres that it was a very fine day. 'I assure you that you will be tired of saying this before many days are over,' replied his lordship.

The trauma of slavery and colonialism

It is impossible to understand the West Indians fully without some knowledge of their history, and in particular of the successive traumas of colonisation, slavery, emancipation and the struggle for independence through which they have passed and which have made them largely what they are today.

From the moment when Christopher Columbus first set foot in the Caribbean in 1492, the region became an integral part of the European power struggle. The Spanish seized the larger islands of the Greater Antilles, Cuba, Hispaniola and Puerto Rico; the French and British concentrated at first on the Lesser Antilles and then on Haiti (France) and Jamaica (Britain); while the Dutch settled on the small Leeward Islands and on the small group of islands off the coast of Venezuela. Even the Danes had some interest in the region for many years until they sold their Virgin Islands in 1917 to the USA. By the mid-eighteenth century every West Indian island was under the control of one or other of the European powers.

What of the original inhabitants? They belonged to two very different races. The gentle Arawaks were forced to work on the new plantations: they succumbed to harsh treatment and disease and were eventually wiped out. The other race, the fierce cannibals called 'Caribs', from whom the region takes its name, resisted bravely but were subdued in time and were either killed or deported to Central America, only one small community of a few hundred surviving in a remote part of Dominica. The West Indians of today are therefore the descendants of people who were all immigrants—usually against their will—and they do not belong to the Caribbean in any ethnic sense.

To work the plantations the Europeans began to import slaves from Africa during the sixteenth century, and so began the notorious 'Triangle Trade': European goods to Africa to be exchanged for slaves and slaves to the West Indies to be exchanged for tobacco, coffee, rum and sugar for selling in Europe. It has been estimated that about 4 million Africans were sold as slaves in the British, French and Dutch territories of the Caribbean, yet when emancipation came in the early nineteenth century, the population of African descent

B

numbered only 1½ million. In the USA, on the other hand, the population of Negroes when slavery came to an end is estimated to have been eleven times the number that had been imported. Although it is now nearly a century and a half since emancipation, the West Indians, white and black, are still suffering the psychological aftermath of the trauma of slavery.

Nearly everywhere emancipation meant simply the substitution of economic servitude for slavery. The West Indies became poverty-stricken islands and an embarrassment to the European powers which still controlled them. Yet for all their poverty the West Indians passionately desired their independence. Haiti had shown the way as far back as 1804 when the Negro slaves threw off their French masters and became the first free Negro republic in the world. In time the larger islands achieved their independence—countries like the Dominican Republic, Jamaica and Trinidad—and in recent years the smaller islands too have been gaining either full independence or at least full control of domestic affairs. The long struggle for independence is still fresh in the minds of West Indians and has played its part in moulding their present character.

Racial origins

The West Indians are overwhelmingly Negro in origin. The only island in which a majority of the population is of European origin is Puerto Rico, where over three-quarters are white, mostly Spanish. The Dominican Republic also has a relatively high proportion of whites, about one-quarter, most of the rest of the people being of mixed ancestry. Trinidad is an exception in that it has a high proportion of East Indians who came to the island as indentured workers during the nineteenth century. About 135,000 East Indians were imported at that time and today they represent nearly half the population. There are also small Asian minorities in

Jamaica and the French Antilles. Several thousand Chinese were brought to the West Indies as indentured workers, mainly to Jamaica, Trinidad and the French Antilles. However, they did not take well to plantation work and tended instead to become small shopkeepers, so that the local grocery store is often called the 'china shop' in the West Indies. In Trinidad a number of Chinese have become very successful market gardeners. The Chinese are dispersed widely over the whole of the West Indies, and in recent years numerous Chinese restaurants have been opened in many West Indian towns and cities. Two other interesting minority groups are the Syrians and the Lebanese, who arrived at the end of the nineteenth century as itinerant pedlars and many of whom have since become prosperous traders.

There has of course been a great deal of intermixing of the races over the years and most of the islands have a substantial proportion of population of mixed blood. The West Indian Negro shows little sign of colour consciousness compared for instance with his brothers and sisters in the USA. This is probably because he has seldom been in a minority group, numerically speaking, and thus has never developed a minority complex or an acute colour consciousness.

As to the white people of the islands, they fall into a number of different categories. At one extreme are the 'poor' whites, such as the 'Redlegs' of Barbados, the 'Cha Chas' of St Thomas, or the 'Blancs Matignons' of the French Antilles. At the other extreme are the longstanding creole families (ie those who have lived in the Caribbean for generations) such as the 'Bekes', an 'hermetic caste' of aristocratic white islanders in Martinique who are acutely colour conscious although they number only 1 per cent of the population. In between are the white people whose ancestors owned plantations or commercial businesses and who are still found mainly in agriculture or commerce; or professional people such as teachers and doctors, who have come out to the West Indies recently and who are unlikely to take up permanent residence. There are also increasing numbers of wealthy

Americans or Europeans who have taken retirement homes in the Caribbean and are living out their days there. In Jamaica and Curaçao there is a small but highly influential community of Jews.

The West Indian Negroes are facing a crisis of identity. They are Africans who have never lived in Africa, speaking European languages and educated in European cultural traditions, living in a part of the world to which their ancestors were brought as slaves against their will. What are they? European, African or American—or some amalgam of all three? Should they, as many of the younger poets and writers urge, strive to understand and take pride in their African origins? Or should they try to forget their African past and build instead a new sense of identity simply as West Indians? It is a dilemma which the people of countries with ancient settled civilisations can hardly begin to comprehend.

Language

Just as there are many races so there are many languages, but nearly all of them are European. The language of the original Amerind people has long since vanished, and as the slaves were forced to speak the languages of their masters so the original African tribal languages have also passed out of use. Thus the lingua franca in each island is the language of the European power which held sway longest. Numerically, Spanish is the language spoken by the largest number of West Indians, because it is the language spoken in the largest islands, the Dominican Republic and Puerto Rico, which together represent over 7 million people. French (or Patois) comes next in importance, thanks to the 5 million or more people in Haiti, followed by English, and then Dutch which is spoken by about 250,000 people. Although Spanish is the first language in Puerto Rico, English was accorded equal status in 1898 following the defeat of the Spanish in the Spanish-American War and the American domination of the country, when a determined but unsuccessful attempt was made to substitute English for Spanish in all the schools: today about a quarter of the Puerto Ricans can speak English and it is the language of commerce.

In some of the islands with a French background a local patois is spoken—notably in Haiti, where only a small educated and wealthy élite can speak French. In Martinique the teachers scorn the patois, and its use in schools is very much discouraged. Yet it has a remarkable capacity to survive, as indeed it has done even in those islands like Dominica which were once French but have been British for two centuries or more. Sometimes an extremely primitive form of patois called 'creole' is spoken; this contains so many words of African origin that even the French people find it almost impossible to understand.

In the islands with a British background there is a marked difference between the kind of English spoken by the educated classes and the whites, and that spoken by the uneducated which makes up in verve and vigour what it lacks in grammatical accuracy. Some of the modern writers and poets use this 'uneducated' English deliberately, as they feel that it captures more accurately the true spirit of West Indian life.

In the Netherlands Antilles the lingua franca is often the compound of Dutch and Spanish called 'Papiamento'. In Trinidad the East Indians have preserved their Hindi language, and the Chinese people also have retained their language.

The population explosion

The population of the West Indies as defined earlier is about $17\frac{1}{2}$ million: it is impossible to be exact, as census statistics are sometimes out of date. Some of the islands are very thickly populated and Barbados, with 1,530 persons per square mile (compared with 570 in Britain) is one of the most densely populated places in the world. However, the

Barbadians must have seen the red light, as the rate of population increase has fallen dramatically and the island now has one of the lowest rates outside Europe. Elsewhere the population explosion continues unabated. Haiti has only 635 persons per square mile on a straight division basis (ie total population divided by total land area), but if one allows for the fact that only 13·7 per cent of the land surface is cultivable, the effective density in the main inhabited parts is nearer 2,000 persons per square mile—and the population is still increasing at a rapid rate. This means tiny patches of land, acute overcrowding and grinding poverty for the 5.4 million people on the island.

The situation is certain to get worse because the West Indies has one of the fastest rates of population growth anywhere in the world—of the order of 3·5 per cent per annum in Jamaica for instance. At present rates of growth the population is likely to be about 36 million by the end of the century. The island governments are aware of the seriousness of the population explosion and are actively encouraging family planning schemes, or, as they call them in Puerto Rico to avoid offending Catholic susceptibilities, 'family spacing' schemes. Trinidad for instance spent £200,000 (about US $500,000) on family planning during the five years up to 1973. These measures are having some success but it will be quite a long time before this is fully reflected in the population statistics, because about half the population in most of the West Indian islands is under twenty-one, and as these young people have their families, so the population is certain to increase sharply. The high proportion of children in the population is a heavy burden for the poorer countries to carry and rural schools and medical services, as will be shown later, are often very rudimentary. The dramatic fall in the death rate, particularly among babies in their first year of life, has been a major factor influencing population increase. In Puerto Rico for example the death rate has fallen from a level of 132.3 per thousand in the 1930s to 5.6 now (compared with 9.5 in the USA).

Religion

Apart from the primitive African religions such as voodoo and obeah, and the Hindu and Islamic faiths practised by the East Indians of Trinidad, the religions of the West Indies are mainly those of Europe and North America. The Negro slaves adopted the religions, as they adopted the speech, of their masters, although in the course of time they introduced many features of their own to 'spice up' the Europeans' rather formal worship, such as religious parades and festivals that evolved into masquerade and carnival, and uninhibited singing and dancing. Roman Catholicism predominated in those territories formerly under the influence of the Spanish or French, and Protestantism prevailed elsewhere. In Trinidad the Roman Catholics, Protestants and Hindu/Moslems roughly balance each other in number.

Voodoo, together with its near neighbour obeah, is of particular interest because of its African origins, and because in recent years some West Indian leaders, anxious to enhance the prestige of everything African, have been urging a re-examination of its merits. Voodoo is strongest in Haiti, where it was one of the mainsprings in the successful revolt of the slaves against French rule. It is a religion or 'cult' of the peasant rather than of the better educated townsman. It protects the poor peasants from a hostile world of spirits and links them to the spirits of their forefathers. Its ceremonies and rituals, the incessant drumming and frenzied dancing, the ecstasy and the spirit-possession, all provide an escape from the grim poverty and monotony of their lives. Voodoo and the Roman Catholic church have always been closely intertwined in Haiti. The Roman Catholic priests (only 113 out of a total of 416 in 1963 were Haitians) have tried to weaken the link, as it is an embarrassment to them, but 'Papa Doc' Duvalier went out of his way to strengthen it as he saw in voodoo a means of contact with the common people that the Roman Catholic church could not provide. As to obeah, this is little more than the African witch-doctor with his charms and spells translated to a Caribbean environment: it involves the casting of spells and such primitive practices as the sprinkling of grave-dust on the chosen victim. It is banned in most West Indian islands, but it is still a force in the more remote rural areas where the people tend to be very superstitious by nature.

The so-called 'folk' religions are very important in the Caribbean where they add a colourful dimension to religious life. They include the Pentecostalists, Seventh Day Adventists, Shango (mainly in Trinidad and Grenada), Pocomania and Rastafari (chiefly in Jamaica) and Shouter (Trinidad). They involve intensive congregational participation and often some degree of spirit-possession or semi-trance state. Some of them, like Rastafari, have strong political undertones.

At the 1960 Census of Population in Trinidad, only 4,375 people out of the 784,000 enumerated stated that they had no religion at all. Unlike the situation in a good number of European countries today, religion still plays a very important part in the lives of most West Indians.

2

How the Countries Are Run

EVER since Haiti became the first Caribbean country to achieve its independence in 1804, the other countries of the region have been striving for independence and for political maturity as self-governing nations.

Haiti

Probably Haiti achieved its independence too early for its own good and it has since paid a high price in terms of economic and political stagnation. A long period of anarchy during the nineteenth and early twentieth centuries was brought to an end by the landing in 1915 of marines from the USA. For a time there was an imposed stability, but the marines departed in 1934, leaving behind little but a few good roads which quickly deteriorated and a fiery resentment at the American intervention. Haiti reverted to its previous isolation and stagnation and it is now one of the poorest and most backward countries in the world.

Under a succession of 'presidents for life', culminating in the cruel regime of 'Papa Doc' Duvalier, Haiti has endured generations of oppression and autocratic rule which have left its people totally unprepared for democratic government. Not that they are in fact likely to have any opportunity to try such a system of government, since Papa Doc's son Jean-Claude Duvalier, known as 'Baby Doc', has declared his intention to perpetuate the Duvalier regime indefinitely.

The president rules with the aid of a Cabinet, but there are no free elections and not even a vestige of representative government.

The impressive public buildings and monuments of Port au Prince, including the Legislative Building and the President's Palace, are no substitute for democracy and serve merely to emphasise the extreme poverty of the great majority of the people who live in the city. And if you stop to admire them for more than a minute or two, an armed guard will soon move you on. If ever there was a place where the reverse of Professor Galbraith's aphorism 'public squalor and private affluence' applies, it is Haiti.

The British West Indies

The other countries of the West Indies followed a less dramatic, but ultimately far more successful, course than Haiti's. The English-speaking countries moved towards independence in a series of stages. Barbados and the Bahamas had a form of parliamentary government with responsibility for domestic affairs from a very early date: Barbados is particularly proud of the fact that its House of Assembly has existed since 1639, while the Bahamas have had a democratically elected House of Assembly since 1792. There was a setback in the slow movement towards independence during Britain's 'Imperial period' in the latter part of the nineteenth century, but progress was resumed after World War I, and now all the larger British islands have gained their independence: Jamaica and Trinidad and Tobago in 1962; Barbados in 1966; and the Bahamas, or to use their correct title, the Commonwealth of the Bahama Islands, in 1973.

Parliamentary institutions, modelled on the British system but with a Senate instead of the House of Lords, are firmly established in all four countries, and in several of them a number of peaceful switches in power between the ruling party and opposition parties have taken place through the polls. These countries, although independent, remain members of the British Commonwealth and they have a governor (now usually a local man) who represents the Queen; the Queen's head also appears on their postage stamps. This is resented by some people in some of the countries, and in Trinidad for instance there is a strong movement to have the country declare itself a republic in the near future; a Constitution Commission was set up in 1973 to consider the type of constitution the people wanted, and in particular whether they preferred a republic. Trinidad is already cultivating close links with Venezuela, and in 1972 the 'Big Four' (Jamaica, Trinidad, Guyana and Barbados) announced their intention to seek closer diplomatic relations with Cuba; Jamaica has also established closer relations with China and has welcomed the establishment of a Chinese embassy in Kingston.

The smaller islands of the British West Indies present a far more intractable problem. They naturally desire independence, but are clearly too small to flourish for long as completely independent units. In the case of Montserrat, with its population of 15,000 people, this is obvious, and in fact it has opted to remain indefinitely as a British colony. The tiny island of Anguilla (6,000 people), following its withdrawal from the federation of St Kitts, Nevis and Anguilla and the landing of British paratroops in 1970, has been accorded similar status. The British Virgin Islands and the Cayman Islands (both with a population of about 10,500) and the Turks and Caicos Islands (5,600 people) are also likely to remain indefinitely as dependent territories of Britain.

The islands that present the most difficult problems politically are the Leeward and Windward Islands. They have populations of the order of 50,000–100,000 and are too large to be satisfied with colonial status, yet they are really too small to justify fully independent nationhood. Some form of federation seems to be the obvious answer, but it has been tried in the past without much success, and the failure of the West Indian Federation of the early 1960s has diminished the chances of a solution being found in this direction. At present they are 'associated states', which means that they have domestic self-rule, but Britain is responsible for defence and foreign policy. This is not a satisfactory solution to Britain, as the Anguilla incident showed, because it puts the British Government in the delicate position of having certain commitments without any real power to find solutions to the problems. It seems likely that the larger islands in these two groups will, in the first instance, seek full independence (Grenada became an independent state in February 1974, and Antigua and St Lucia will probably follow suit later), but that in due course they will seek some loose form of association like that entered into recently by Grenada, St Vincent and St Lucia which provides for free movement of labour and other links of a similar sort.

The Spanish Antilles

The largest Spanish-speaking country in the West Indies, the Dominican Republic, achieved its independence from Spain in 1894. This was much earlier than the British islands, but, as with Haiti, the republic was ill prepared for independence or democratic government. Parliamentary government never took proper root and the country was ruled by a succession of autocrats. Between 1844 and 1930 the country had forty-three presidents and fifty-six revolutions! Chaos and political turmoil reached such a pitch that in 1916 the USA, prompted partly by strategic considerations, intervened to establish law and order. American marines remained for eight years, and for a few years after their departure there was some stability, but then the Great Slump in America in 1929 and its economic consequences in the Caribbean led to the emergence of yet another dictator—worse even than those who had gone before—Molina Trujillo. He governed the country with utter ruthlessness for many years until he was assassinated in 1961. There followed another period of unrest verging on civil war, but in 1966 a new constitution was introduced, modelled on the American system with a

president and Congress, and since then the political situation
has been stabilised considerably. President Balaguer is right-
wing, and was once an aide of Trujillo, but he enjoys
the support of the USA (which fears above all another Cuba
in the Caribbean) and the country's economy is benefiting
from the flow of American investment and aid. What will
happen however when President Balaguer goes, is highly
uncertain, and a reversion to political instability is very
likely. The tender plant of democracy in the Dominican
Republic still has shallow roots.

The other large Spanish-speaking country, Puerto Rico, has
achieved less progress towards independence than any other
large Caribbean state, but on the other hand it has made the
greatest economic progress. The island was ceded by Spain to
the USA by the Treaty of Paris in 1898, after four centuries
of Spanish rule. For years it was in a depressed condition and
its people emigrated in large numbers to the USA following
the grant of American citizenship in 1917. However, during
the 1940s, the country's economy was given a boost under the
leadership of Munoz Marin, and in 1952 the political situation was stabilised when Puerto Rico was granted a new
constitution and became a 'Commonwealth Associated with
the United States'. The constitution provides for a governor
elected by direct referendum, a Cabinet, a Senate and a
House of Representatives. Puerto Ricans also elect a com-
missioner to represent them in the United States House of
Representatives, but he has no vote. The island thus has a
very curious status. Puerto Ricans can be conscripted into the
American army, have American passports and can move freely
to and from the USA. But they cannot determine their own
foreign policy and they have to put up with such minor provo-
cations as that of an air hostess reminding passengers about to
land at San Juan that they will need visas as Puerto Rico is
'a possession of the United States'. Yet their unique status
has undoubtedly brought remarkable economic benefits and
the island now has one of the highest standards of living in
the Caribbean, a gross national product of £658 (US $1,648)

per head of population, compared with Haiti's £44 (US $110). Many of the million or more Puerto Ricans who emigrated to the USA during the depressed years, and their families, are now returning to their homeland. The Puerto Ricans themselves are rather divided as to whether they want the present system with its economic advantages to remain indefinitely, or whether they would prefer independence. Pride pulls them towards independence, but their pockets pull the other way: many indeed would prefer to go the whole hog and have full statehood within the USA. For the time being it seems that the pocket will prevail, but at the elections in 1972 the pro-Commonwealth party replaced the pro-Statehood party and this may be a straw in the wind. Ultimately some movement towards independence seems likely. The USA has indicated its willingness to accept either solution and it is now up to the Puerto Ricans themselves to decide.

The French Antilles

The French islands of Martinique and Guadeloupe and their smaller dependencies have chosen the Puerto Rican road of economic growth at the expense of political independence, and since 1946 have been full Departments of France. The people are free to move at will to and from France; they enjoy the same social security services as the people of France; they are full members of the European Economic Community; and they receive very high prices for their sugar and rum in the protected French market. They send six members altogether to the National Assembly, and four to the Senate. The status of these islands is a major impediment to plans for a wider federation of the West Indian islands, particularly as regards the Leeward and Windward Islands.

The Netherlands Antilles

The Dutch islands of Aruba, Bonaire and Curaçao (sometimes called the 'ABC' islands), together with the smaller islands of St Martin (shared with the French), Saba and St Eustatius in the Leeward Islands (which the Dutch call, confusingly, the Windward Islands), have a status rather similar to that of the French islands. They are an integral part of the kingdom of the Netherlands, and the people are full Dutch citizens. However, they have been given full autonomy in local affairs and only issues of defence or foreign policy are handled by the Netherlands Government. The Dutch Leeward Islands send one member to the Staten of twenty-two members in Curaçao. Although their population is less than that of a typical British city, the Netherlands Antilles have no less than eight political parties, and politics are convoluted and parochial in the extreme.

Severe riots occurred in 1969 in Willemstad, capital of Curaçao and these have led to a movement for the ultimate granting of independence. A Dutch Royal Commission has been sitting to consider this issue. However, as with the Windward Islands, the basic problem is that these islands, apart from Curaçao and possibly Aruba, are too small to qualify for full independence from each other and therefore some kind of federation of the Dutch possessions in the West Indies, or perhaps a 'Commonwealth', is being discussed as a stepping-stone to independence some time in the future. From the recent reactions of the island governments to these proposals, however, it seems clear that an effective federation will be no easier to achieve here than it has been elsewhere in the Caribbean. The main problem is that the small Dutch islands in the Leewards have very little in common with their wealthy cousins in the 'ABC' countries.

These islands have increasingly valuable oil refineries, and if they secured complete independence they could be at the mercy of some larger state which decided to intervene to prevent a power vacuum developing as a result of the departure of Dutch military and naval units . . . and to seize the oil installations. Remote as it may seem at present, this is a factor which the leaders of the Netherlands Antilles cannot altogether dismiss. Another anxiety is that full independence would mean the end of the right which the people at present enjoy of living and working in the Netherlands, a very important privilege in view of the high rate of unemployment in the islands. So independence has a price, and the local politicians are making haste slowly.

The American Virgin Islands

These were owned by Denmark until 1917 when the USA bought them, largely for strategic reasons. They are now technically colonies of the USA but they have local autonomy in domestic affairs. They have become a favourite tourist centre, and many retirement homes have been built there.

FAILURE OF FEDERATION

After World War II the British Government revived an earlier idea of a federation of the British West Indies and put its full weight behind the realisation of this. In 1958, after the Montego Bay Conference had laid the foundations, the West Indies Federation was established. It was a federation of

———

New government offices, Roseau, Dominica

The Red House Parliament Building, Port of Spain, Trinidad

all the British islands in the Caribbean and was indeed a bold initiative. But it was many years ahead of its time. None of the participating states had yet achieved independence and the larger ones joined the Federation partly because they hoped it might speed up their progress towards full independence. When Jamaica and Trinidad realised that they could have full independence immediately if they pushed hard enough, they were no longer interested in the Federation, which in any case had proved itself powerless to govern in any effective way since it could not levy taxes and had little executive authority. Moreover it was never able to overcome the problem of distance and poor communications over the 1,250 miles which the islands span. Then again, Jamaica and Trinidad were afraid that they would have to subsidise the smaller, poorer islands and provide jobs for the workless so that in the end the Federation would be merely a 'pooling of poverty'.

Jamaica withdrew from the Federation in 1961 and Trinidad a year later ('One taken from ten leaves zero', said Dr Eric Williams, Prime Minister of Trinidad and Tobago). The great experiment was over: the recriminations had only just begun. In the years that followed, various attempts were

---

San Juan Market, near Port of Spain, Trinidad

Shanty housing on the outskirts of Port of Spain

made to establish lesser federations of the smaller islands, but they came to nothing. The most promising, however, and so far the most successful, has been the limited agreement between Grenada, St Vincent and St Lucia mentioned earlier. Under this agreement, nationals of the three islands can move freely among them without permits or passports, and may own land on any of them. These are limited steps in the direction of union, but because they do not require the surrender of autonomy, they are more likely to succeed than more ambitious schemes in the present climate of opinion. Political federation of the British West Indies as a whole is now a dead duck, but schemes for local integration and economic co-operation are still very much alive. Two of the most successful examples of the 'federal' idea working in the economic field are the Caribbean Common Market, which has grown out of the Caribbean Free Trade Area (CARIFTA), and the Caribbean Development Bank.

POLITICAL LIFE

Universal suffrage, usually from the age of eighteen (or in some countries twenty-one), is the pattern in most of the West Indian islands, and there is a very active political life. There are often many small parties, and political issues are taken very seriously.

Most of the political parties represent labour in one form or another; there are very few right-wing parties of major significance except in the Dominican Republic, and few extreme left-wing parties except in Martinique where the communists are strong. Because they are striving frequently for the same broad ends, often advocating virtually the same means, the parties tend to polarise around personalities and they often have a short life, merging and splintering and merging again as they search for electoral advantages or as candidates change. While independence was the principal goal, party loyalties had a natural focal point, but since the achievement of independence the political barometer has

moved in a less predictable manner. In Trinidad and Tobago
Dr Eric Williams, leader of the People's National Movement,
is under heavy attack because of what are considered to be
his 'conservative' policies, and at the 1971 elections the opposition parties boycotted the polls completely so that more than
half the electorate was effectively disenfranchised. Jamaica
has basically a two-party system. The 1972 elections ended the
long rule of the Jamaican Labour Party and brought into
power Mr Michael Manley, son of Mr Norman Manley, and
his People's National Party. Mr Manley's declaration on
taking office is typical of the deep roots which the English
democratic system has put down in the Caribbean: 'My own
commitment to the democratic process is absolutely fundamental, and it is a profound thing with me.' In the French
islands political life is at a rather low ebb because the islands
are too small to have much influence on the results of the
French elections. In Puerto Rico the issue of the country's
relations with the USA dominates political life, while in the
Dominican Republic, almost alone among Caribbean countries, the main political issues centre round whether the
economy should evolve along a socialistic or capitalistic path.
In Haiti there is no political life worthy of the name. Instead
the nation is divided into two groups that are so profoundly
different from each other that J. G. Leyburn the anthropologist, in his perceptive book *The Haitian People* (1966)
called them 'castes'. On the one hand is the small élitist urban
minority, French-speaking, often wealthy, well educated and
of white or mixed blood: and on the other hand are the great
majority of the people, the very poor, largely illiterate patois-
speaking peasants, from whom the Duvaliers have drawn their
support. Politics in Haiti is mainly represented by the
struggle between these two 'castes'.

The long period of unrest and civil disturbance in Trinidad before and during Carnival 1970, with window-smashing,
riots and an army mutiny, and which led to the declaration
of a state of emergency, brought into the limelight the
growing strength of the Black Power movement and sent

ripples of anxiety throughout the Caribbean islands. It was only the steadfastness of the police that averted more serious trouble in Trinidad, and even so another state of emergency had to be declared from October 1971 to June 1972.

Trinidad is not the only Caribbean country to have experienced Black Power. The 1960 riots in Kingston, Jamaica were expressions of racial unrest as well as a protest against unemployment and poor housing. Visitors are still strongly advised not to walk at night through West Kingston and shootings are everyday occurrences. The 1968 riots there were associated more directly with Black Power, particularly Marcus Garvey's 'Back to Africa' movement. In its early days this movement was related more to 'Black Nationalism', ie a rediscovery of the positive virtues of the African culture and way of life, and it was only in recent years that it became politically associated with the Black Power movement. Nor have the smaller islands been immune. Antigua has had some quite serious riots, while in the Bahamas the government's attempts to restrain immigration at Freeport led to Black Power-inspired opposition. In Dominica the protest of young Black Power adherents led to the temporary closing of one of the island's leading schools in 1972. There have also been incidents in Puerto Rico where the separatist movement draws active support from Black Power.

GOVERNMENT AND SECURITY

The civil service and local government

One of the most enduring legacies of the European powers in most of the islands was an efficient civil service. Lord Balogh, formerly economic adviser to the British Cabinet, has commented that the calibre of top civil servants in Jamaica was as high as that of their counterparts in Britain or indeed anywhere else. The civil servants in all the British West Indian islands have a high reputation for their honesty and on the whole their efficiency, although the usual complaints of bureaucracy are heard everywhere. The civil service in these islands is usually run on British lines, and hitherto salaries have been reasonably high so that the best men have been attracted into the service; but recently commerce and industry have become more competitive and this has been a cause for concern. The civil servants journey quite frequently to Britain on official business, or to other islands in the Caribbean, so they are often well informed and much travelled. The French islands also have a very efficient civil service and a unique feature there is that the civil servants can qualify on promotion for posts in France exactly on a par with Frenchmen. In Puerto Rico there has been a great improvement in the status and efficiency of the civil service in recent years in parallel with the economic development of the country, but the Dominican Republic and Haiti have suffered from civil services that have been both as inefficient and as subject to corruption as the regimes they have had to serve, although the situation is now improving.

So far as local government is concerned, the pattern is that in the larger islands a well-developed form of local government has evolved to meet the needs of the towns and villages, but the main power is very much concentrated in the hands of the central local government. In the smaller islands there is as yet virtually no local government system, although in some of them attempts have been made recently to institute village councils and town councils on an elective basis to administer certain local services and to act as a training-ground for representative government on the larger scale.

Legal systems and police

The legal system in those islands with a British background is based on English common law, and hitherto most training in law has been given in England. However, there is a general movement to 'West Indianise' the legal system, and in 1971 the Legal Profession Act was introduced in the Jamaican Parliament. This Act merges barristers and solicitors under one common profession to be called simply 'attorneys'; it also provides for a General Legal Council to supervise legal training and the profession generally. There is too a proposal to establish a regional Court of Appeal to replace the Judicial Committee of the Privy Council. The law is a very lucrative profession in the West Indies, as in most places, and because of the vast number of territorial disputes resulting from the inadequate records of land ownership in the past, the lawyer is seldom without clients.

In the French and Dutch islands the legal system is modelled on that of the parent country; in the Dominican Republic it is based on the Spanish system; in Puerto Rico the situation is rather complicated, as most cases are still tried on the basis of Roman or civil law despite the fact that a great deal of the Anglo-Saxon legal system has now been adopted.

To enforce the law, each island has its own police force, that on the British Commonwealth islands being modelled on the British system (for instance the policemen do not carry guns); and the others on the police forces of France, the Netherlands or the USA. Jamaica has a police force of 84 officers and 3,050 men for a population of about 2 million people. At one time this would have been perfectly adequate to maintain law and order, but today the police force in Jamaica, as in most of the islands, is under great pressure. Twenty years ago the most common offence was one that is virtually unknown today in Europe or the USA—praedial larceny, or the stealing of growing crops. Policemen from the West Indies sent to Britain for training were astonished to find that their instructors hardly knew the meaning of the word. But in the last two decades, with increasing affluence and sophistication, praedial larceny has diminished and has been replaced by more serious crimes and by a rapid increase in motoring offences. Crime is now one of the major problems on most of the islands, particularly those with high unemployment. In Trinidad for instance cases of serious crime handled by the police rose by 10 per cent per annum during the period

1960–7. In Jamaica the murder rate increased 70 per cent between 1962/3 and 1966/7: all the houses in the affluent Beverley Hills area of Kingston have bars across the windows, and most of them display 'Beware of the dog' signs. The *Economist* in 1970 declared that Kingston had become 'the most dangerous city on earth'. If there is a commotion in the street and you ask the taxi-driver what is afoot, he will reply casually: 'It's probably another shooting.' In the American Virgin Islands, where crime was once almost unknown, a recent report described the people as 'racked with fear' because of the crime wave.

A sinister recent development is that political protest movements are beginning to take a violent form. It is not unusual these days for the Trinidad police to have to fight small pitched battles with Marxist guerrillas of the 'National United Freedom Fighters' in the forests and mountains of the Northern Range. Three police-stations were shot up and several policemen killed during 1973.

Attitudes to the police vary from island to island, but in general it can be said that they are more tolerated than liked. The people certainly do not think of them as the British think of their local 'bobby'. The great majority of the policemen, except in Puerto Rico and the French Antilles, are Negroes, even in Trinidad where nearly half the population are East Indians (but only 3 per cent are in the police force). In the French Antilles a high proportion of the gendarmerie is Algerian or European, a fact that is much resented there. Even where the police are Negroes, there is a tendency to regard them as the latter-day symbols of colonialist power. The police are always thought to be on the side of the influential or wealthy and down on the poor and oppressed. If a wealthy man breaks the law it is widely expected that the police will seldom prosecute, but if a poor man transgresses he suffers the full penalty. This attitude may be due in part to the general feeling among West Indians that the law is an alien thing—something opposed to their traditional ways of life and living patterns; and it may be due in part to the fact that the police themselves are often overworked and under-paid and are not always well educated. In an endeavour to improve relations between the police and the public the Jamaican police force in 1973 decided to set up a new Press Relations Council, and this is certainly a step in the right direction.

In Puerto Rico the police wear similar uniforms to those worn by their counterparts in the USA and they are also armed. They look very tough compared with the police in Jamaica and the other islands of the British Commonwealth, where shorts and white pith helmets are still worn. The police in Haiti are virtually the private army of the president. 'Papa Doc' Duvalier created the feared 'Ton Ton Macoutes' (creole for 'bogeymen') a force of some 10,000 security police under the president's personal control. The presidential palace is an arsenal for this private army (some of the ammu-nition exploded in the basement in 1973 and the young Duvalier was nearly killed) and still today the palace is defended by tanks and anti-aircraft guns. The police can be seen drilling in the forecourt in military style. The Ton Ton Macoutes were disbanded a few years ago and replaced by the 'Leopards' but it was more a change of name than of substance.

As to national defence, only the larger territories in the Caribbean have their own armed forces; in the smaller islands the pattern is for the police to be supplied with military equipment so that they can deal effectively with serious internal disorders, the respective European powers being responsible for external defence. Jamaica, however, has an efficient little army modelled on British lines and based on the old British army camp in the centre of Kingston. Haiti has a small army of about 5,000 men trained by the USA and which was in action in 1973 when it repelled an abortive attempt by a group of guerrillas to invade the country. Puerto Rico of course does not require an army because it is part of the USA. The Dominican Republic has a small army which is used to preserve internal security and to deter any attempt at invasion. It was also in action in 1973 when a small band of political rebels entered the territory illegally. It is one of the anxieties of the USA that the two countries of Hispaniola (Haiti and the Dominican Republic) have so little capacity to defend themselves against determined attack from outside— say from Cuba, and American foreign policy in the West Indies is much influenced by this preoccupation. Not so long ago there was enmity between Haiti and the Dominican Republic and the armies of each country were largely engaged in patrolling the frontier, but today there is less tension and the possibility of a threat from outside, however remote, has served to bring them closer together.

TRADE, FINANCE AND TAXATION

Trade

Nearly all the West Indian islands have been traditionally export economies; they grow tropical crops such as sugar, bananas, citrus fruits, tobacco and coffee, for sale mainly to the USA, Europe or Japan, either as the raw product or in processed form such as fruit juice, cigars, or rum. If they are lucky they also have mineral products to sell, such as petro-leum (Trinidad), bauxite—the raw material of aluminium (Jamaica) or nickel (Dominican Republic). The other large 'export' they have is tourism, which is particularly useful because the 'goods' (ie beaches, seas for sailing in, mountain-ous landscapes, etc) do not have to be shipped abroad; instead the customers have to come and consume them themselves.

As for the imports these tend to be, as one might expect, mainly manufactured goods of all kinds, again largely from the USA, Europe or Japan but, more surprisingly, they also include a substantial proportion of food. Food has to be imported partly because the people have chosen to grow export crops in preference to vegetables and cereals, and partly because the tourists generally prefer to eat in the hotels the kind of food to which they are accustomed, such as corn-flakes and steaks, and often these are not produced on the islands.

The following table of imports and exports for St Kitts and Nevis is typical of the pattern in the smaller West Indian islands:

Imports and Exports, St Kitts and Nevis, 1970 (EC $ million)

Imports		Exports	
Food	6.38	Sugar and molasses	6.63
Manufactures	5.13	Other	1.59
Machinery and transport	4.42		
Miscellaneous	7.50		
Total	23.43	Total	8.22

(The EC $ is worth about half the US $, ie about 20p)

It will be noted that imports greatly exceed exports. To some extent the balance is made up by tourism, which is becoming important on St Kitts, but mainly it is made up by grants and loans from outside, especially by overseas aid from Britain.

Trinidad and Tobago's pattern of imports and exports reflects the extent to which petroleum has ousted the traditional agricultural exports. This pattern would be typical also of Curaçao, and to a lesser extent of Jamaica with its bauxite and aluminium instead of petroleum.

Imports and Exports, Trinidad and Tobago, 1972
(T/T $ million)

Imports		Exports	
Oil products (mainly crude oil from Saudi Arabia and Libya for refining)	702	Petroleum products	832
		Sugar and other food products	92
		Chemicals	78

Machinery and transport		Other	67
	252		
Manufactures	196		
Food	127		
Other	171		
Total	1,448	Total	1,069

(The T/T $ is worth about half the US $, ie about 20p)

Puerto Rico has developed a wider range of industries than the other West Indian islands and this is reflected in its trade figures. Haiti and the Dominican Republic, however, have had very little industrial development and therefore agricultural products continue to dominate their exports and manufactures their imports.

Currency and budgets

Apart from the gourde in Haiti, the peso oro in the Dominican Republic, the franc in the French Antilles and the florin in the Dutch islands, the common currency in the West Indies is the dollar. But, confusingly, the various dollars do not have the same value and this can make life difficult for the unwary traveller. The dollar used in the East Caribbean and in Trinidad and Tobago is worth about half the American dollar, but the Jamaican dollar is worth a little more than the American. Because of their traditional dependence on export crops the currencies of most of the West Indian islands have been tied to those of the parent European country, or to the USA as the case may be. The Windward and Leeward Islands, Barbados and the British Virgin Islands belong to the Eastern Caribbean Currency Union, but there is a real possibility that Barbados will soon set up its own central bank and will then leave the Union. Jamaica decided to cut loose from sterling in 1972 and devalued its dollar.

As one would expect of countries which have so much leeway to make up after years of poverty, a high proportion of recurrent expenditure in the national budgets is devoted to the social services, especially schools, hospitals and communications. Jamaica's 1971 budget is fairly typical of the other islands in the region:

Budget Expenditure, Jamaica, 1971 (Jamaican $ million)

Recurrent Expenditure		Capital Expenditure	
Education	33.4	Communications	
Local government	25.0	and roads	21.3
Health	24.8	Finance	17.6
Communications and		Local government	11.6
roads	20.8	Other	42.8
Home affairs	13.7		
Finance (ie to meet the government's financial commitments at home and overseas)	61.0		
Other	42.3		
Total	221.0	Total	93.3

(The J $ is worth slightly more than the US $, ie about 46p)

Taxation

The main source of revenue to the government in the West Indies, as elsewhere, is taxation. In some of the smaller islands —the Bahamas are a case in point—the government receives such a substantial part of its revenue from import and export duties that it can afford to give important tax remissions to potential investors. Other islands also do this, as shown below, but for all the larger territories direct taxation is the principal source of government revenue. The main forms of direct taxation are income tax, land tax and taxes on the transfer of property; while car licences, stamp duties and the like have become important in recent years. Puerto Rico is in a unique position. Because the country has no vote in the United States House of Representatives, the USA acting on the principle of 'no vote, no taxation', has declared that no federal taxes need be paid by firms operating in Puerto Rico. This has given a great boost to industrial development there since World War II. Trinidad and Tobago introduced purchase tax in 1963, and gambling is also taxed in the form of a pinball tax and pools-betting duty. Barbados has had income tax since 1927 and Pay As You Earn (PAYE) since 1957: the number of taxpayers increased from 10,300 in 1965 to 29,600 in 1970, and the tax revenue from EC $12.7 million to EC $28.6 million. In the mainly peasant-based agricultural countries like Haiti and the Dominican Republic, income tax is still only a small source of government revenue (one-fifth in the Dominican Republic) and these countries continue to depend largely upon customs duties and levies of various kinds.

The efficiency with which income taxes are collected varies a great deal. In Trinidad and Tobago the government recently appointed ten field officers to conduct a door-to-door campaign to collect tax arrears. Jamaica in 1970 tightened up its income tax arrangements to make evasion more difficult and total tax revenue from this source rose in one year by one-third! Judging by the way in which the wealthier people flaunt their cars and expensive villas, there is still a long way to go to make the tax system really effective.

Most Caribbean countries give tax reliefs of various kinds as an incentive to businessmen to develop new industries and particularly tourism, and some attempts have been made recently to harmonise these incentives. In some of the smaller islands, however, the principle of tax incentives has been carried to such an extreme degree that they have come to be called 'tax havens'. Often new industries are relieved of all taxes for a period of years. In a sense, as already mentioned, Puerto Rico is probably the most successful example of a tax haven in the West Indies, but it is a special case and is not really comparable with the tax havens in the small islands. Of these the Cayman Islands is the best known example. This tiny group of islands, with a population of only 10,650, has no less than 3,500 'offshore' companies registered there as well as eighty-five banks, and about fifty telex machines or one for every 200 people—a world record. Only seven years ago the islands could muster only twenty telephones between them; today they have 2,500 and one can dial virtually any country in the world from the Cayman Islands. The government draws more than half its revenue from the island's role as a tax haven. The other main tax havens in the region are the Bahamas (where Freeport is the prime example), the Netherlands Antilles and the British Virgin Islands. Thus of the twelve tax havens in the world at large, four are in the West Indies. In addition there is a number of other territories which give special tax concessions over and above the normal incentives, and these include the Turks and Caicos Islands, St Lucia, Haiti and the American Virgin Islands.

Private overseas investment and aid

The figures of imports and exports given earlier indicate that some at least of the islands have a severe deficit on their visible balance of trade. To some extent, as mentioned earlier, tourist earnings and remittances from abroad help the balance of payments, but generally the gap is made up by heavy inflows of private capital and overseas aid. Jamaica for instance received massive injections of capital during the 1960s as its bauxite resources were developed by large private companies, but when the pace of development slackened in 1972 and the inflow of private capital diminished suddenly, it quickly found itself in balance-of-payments difficulties and was forced to devalue.

The islands of the British Commonwealth received £27.2 million (about US $67 million) of British aid during 1971, £23.9 million of it in the form of financial grants (£10.5 million) and loans (£13.4 million), and the rest as technical assistance. This aid is administered by the British Development Division in Bridgetown, Barbados. In addition, the Commonwealth Development Corporation in 1972 committed £27 million. The French and the Dutch also give substantial aid to their islands, while the Canadians and Americans and the World Bank have major investment programmes in the region. Haiti has so far received the least aid in proportion to its size and poverty. President Kennedy cut off American aid in 1963 because of the blatant misuse of funds. However, under the new regime of Jean-Paul Duvalier, American-Haitian relations have much improved and the flow of aid to Haiti has been increased. The flow of aid from all quarters to the West Indies makes it one of the world's most heavily aided regions, which is only fitting when one considers the tragedy of slavery which the region suffered in times gone by.

3

How They Live

POVERTY AND AFFLUENCE

THERE are few areas of the world that exhibit greater ranges of income than are found in and between most West Indian islands. Poverty and affluence exist side by side almost everywhere. At one extreme is Haiti. With an income per head of about £44 (US $110) compared with £1,000 (approximately US $2,500) in Britain and £1,905 ($5,000) in the USA, life is reduced to the barest essentials, as a short walk round the teeming city of Port au Prince, where water, sanitation, space, indeed virtually all the necessities of life are desperately short, will soon prove. Only Calcutta, in the author's experience,

———

Spanish influence in architecture, Old San Juan, Puerto Rico

The modern quarter of Port au Prince and the cathedral, Haiti

can match Port au Prince for urban destitution and squalor—apart of course from the affluent areas and the fine public buildings.

At the other extreme are islands like the Caymans, the Netherlands Antilles and the Bahamas, and more recently Puerto Rico, where there is a fairly high standard of living and some pockets of real affluence. All these islands have average per capita incomes exceeding £400 (about US $1,000) per annum, and in such districts as Nassau's Bay Street there are usually two cars outside the house, people dress for dinner, and one can find a sprinkling of British knights and American film stars—especially in the winter months. A taxi-driver in Nassau can easily make £80 (about US $200) per week.

Between the extremes are countries like Jamaica, Trinidad and Barbados, with average net incomes per capita around £280 (US $600) to £360 (US $900) per person per annum, and the islands of the Leewards and Windwards and the Dominican Republic with incomes around £120 to £160 per head.

These averages tend of course to hide some wide ranges. Only a few miles, but probably £800 per head per annum, separate the affluent Montego Bay district of Jamaica from

———

The market square, St George's, Grenada

Broad Street, Bridgetown, Barbados

the nearby 'Cockpit Country', where the descendants of escaped slaves (the 'maroons') still eke out an existence in extreme poverty. In Kingston and in Port of Spain the contrasts are even more obvious. In Puerto Rico, San Juan is a chic modern city, but only a few miles away are villages that have hardly been affected by the economic revolution of the last two decades. This picture could be multiplied a thousand times. In part it is a contrast between town and country; in Trinidad the average net income per household in 1970 was T/T $378 in the urban areas, but only T/T $248 in the rural areas: but even more important, it is also a matter of employment prospects. In the Netherlands Antilles there are lucrative jobs in the oil industry, in Jamaica in bauxite, and in the Bahamas and elsewhere in tourism, while in most of the islands the government employees have been able to maintain a reasonable livelihood. In the rural areas, however, jobs are scarce and wages are usually low. Often the most affluent areas contain a high proportion of expatriates and there is an increasing number of estates occupied almost exclusively by white retired people, such as the Cap Estate in St Lucia with its golf-course and marina.

The range in incomes and standards of living has widened during the last two decades because of the way in which rapid economic development seems to have hit some islands and bypassed others. The classic case of rapid economic growth is Puerto Rico, where the income per head in 1940 was only $120; today it is over $1,000 and double the average income for Latin America as a whole. Jamaica also enjoyed a rapid rate of growth during the 1950s and early 1960s, but the expansion was concentrated largely in the mineral and tourist sectors and the sugar and banana industries did not benefit at all. Income differentials in Jamaica were greatly increased during this period; and the gap between rich and poor is now said to be among the largest of any country in the world. The top 5 per cent of people in the income 'league' earn 30 per cent of the total national income, and the bottom 20 per cent only 2 per cent. In Trinidad, where oil has been the main factor boosting incomes, one-sixth of the workers earn over T/T $300 per month, while one-quarter earn less than T/T $50. Perhaps a certain degree of distortion of this kind is inevitable when economies are developing rapidly and in a selective way, but when the disparity gets too great the political tensions become dangerous and a more equitable distribution of the national income is an urgent priority.

HOUSING

The typical West Indian house is a detached single-storey building of wood with a corrugated iron roof (normal in the West Indies and not itself a sign of poverty) set in its own small plot or 'yard'. Invariably it will have a verandah on at least two sides and it is here, rather than inside the house, that the family will relax in the shade. Few houses as yet have air-conditioning and they are often like ovens in the heat of the day. Rain-water collected from the roof is an important source of water, although most houses are now connected to water-supplies—at least in the towns. The windows are generally fitted with louvres or jalousies. Semi-detached houses or terrace-houses are hardly ever found in the Caribbean, although 'town houses' are making their appearance in the chic urban developments, and flats also are relatively rare except in the larger towns. The French influence can be seen in the large blocks of flats which dot the hillsides around the cities of Martinique and Guadeloupe. Even in the most desperately crowded cities the West Indian family usually contrives to occupy a house of its own, albeit in very cramped and insanitary conditions.

In recent years the tendency has been to build houses of concrete blocks. Brick construction is extremely rare except in those few localities where bricks were brought out from Britain as ballast in sailing ships and were used for the construction of churches and public buildings—there are excellent examples in Spanish Town, Jamaica and in St

George's, Grenada. Solidly built houses have the great advantage of being resistant to hurricanes and fires, the twin scourges of many a West Indian town and village. Castries, St Lucia was almost entirely destroyed by fire just after World War II, and scarcely an old building can be found in Kingston, Jamaica because of the many fires. The fire-engine is a most important piece of civic equipment in the West Indies.

As with standards of living, there is a wide range in the quality of housing in the West Indies. As usual, Haiti represents one extreme. Outside the few towns one finds mostly mud and wattle houses with thatched roofs, and inside the towns a few flamboyant French 'old colonial'-style houses surrounded by a sea of ugly shanties with decaying woodwork and rusty corrugated iron from which flows a daily tide of refuse, excrement, urine and water that has caused Port au Prince to be described as 'the sewer of the Caribbean'. Here and there modern, solidly constructed houses are appearing on the outskirts of the city, but as yet no determined attempts have been made to clear the slums. One can find equally bad pockets of poverty in Port of Spain or in Kingston, Jamaica but there they are the exception rather than the rule.

At the other end of the scale there are development schemes in the Cayman Islands, such as Caymans Kai and North Sound, where a typical house might cost £15,000. More representative of the West Indies generally, however, would be housing in Barbados, and the following statistics from the 1970 Census give a good indication of the housing situation there:

Housing in Barbados

Total number of households: 59,266

Houses	Households with separate houses	55,714
	Households with flats or apartments	2,909
	Other households	643
		59,266

Housing in Barbados—continued

Households owning their houses/flats	43,536
Households renting their houses/flats	11,734
Other	3,996
	59,266

Rooms Households with:

1 room	1,453
2 rooms	8,815
3 rooms	11,382
4 rooms	22,447
5 rooms	9,411
6 or more rooms	3,923
Not known	1,835
	59,266

Construction (outer walls)

Households with houses built of:

Wood	45,081
Concrete	5,730
Stone	5,014
Brick	700
Wood and concrete	2,641
Other	100
	59,266

Fuel *For cooking*		*For lighting*	
Number of households using:		Number of households using:	
Kerosene	41,104	Electricity	35,102
Gas	15,707	Kerosene	24,164
Other	2,455		
	59,266		59,266

It will be observed that the great majority of households were living in separate houses, and they were mostly owner-occupiers. However, these statistics hide the fact that in many cases people did not own the land on which their houses stood, and it is insecurity of tenure of land that often explains the poor state of the houses in the West Indies; householders are simply not prepared to spend money in maintaining and improving their dwellings if they do not own the land on which the houses stand. The typical house had four rooms, was built of wood and lit by electricity, but kerosene was the usual fuel for cooking and was also used for lighting in some cases. A survey in 1968 showed that nearly three-quarters of the houses in Barbados had gardens or 'yards' (a more aptly descriptive word as lawns and flower-beds are relatively rare). The general picture suggested by these statistics would be fairly typical of the rural parts of most islands in the West Indies, and of a good many of the towns too.

Because of the general poverty of the West Indies at the end of World War II, the poor stock of housing at that time and the rapid increase in population in the last twenty years, the provision of housing has failed to keep pace with the demand, and the housing situation has become one of the biggest social problems in the region. Nearly all the islands have major programmes for the building of low-cost and medium-cost houses, sometimes on a massive scale. Trinidad's National Housing Authority has a scheme to house 130,000 people east of Port of Spain, while Jamaica has a Ministry of Housing which has several large housing projects under way to get rid of the squatters' shanties, or 'taboos' as they are called. These include a 'site and services' scheme in Kingston which is very much a pioneering development and may point the way to a breakthrough in the housing bottle-neck: under this scheme the government provides the site and basic services, water, sewerage, roads and possibly the core of the house, while the buyer completes the house to meet his own needs in the way he wishes. In the Bahamas the government is aware of the urgent need to provide more low-cost housing and has a current programme for over 1,000 such houses. The Puerto Rican Government has carried out a major housing development at San José near San Juan, and the *el fanguitos* (little mud-holes) are being bulldozed into extinction. There is a programme currently under way for the building of 123,000 houses.

A relatively recent phenomenon is the building of retirement homes as mentioned earlier. In some cases these developments are actively encouraged by the government, as at Frigate Bay in St Kitts where the policy is to diversify out of sugar at all costs, but sometimes they are frowned upon because in the long run it is not conducive to political stability to allow foreigners to own a substantial part of the land, especially the most favoured beaches. In Antigua the situation has deteriorated to the point where high wire fences have been erected round the most affluent ' compounds ' and there is a guard at the entrance day and night. Trinidad has passed an Aliens Land Holding Act to deter foreigners from acquiring land, while in other islands, such as Jamaica and Barbados, discriminating taxes have been introduced for the same purpose (although these have not deterred a private development company recently from turning a 1,300-acre sugar estate at Montego Bay into an estate for 2,000 luxury villas). In the British Virgin Islands a private company was allowed to reclaim a large part of the foreshore of Roadtown, the tiny capital, but then the government decided to intervene and to acquire the land that had been reclaimed. The issue was taken to the British House of Lords and eventually adequate compensation was agreed. This incident illustrates that even in the smallest islands it is fast becoming politically inexpedient to permit too great a degree of foreign ownership of land, and this is likely to become even more true in the future.

THE DRIFT TO THE CITIES

In common with other regions of the world which are moving from agriculture-based economies to mixed economies, the West Indies in recent years has been experiencing the familiar drift to the cities.

Only twenty-five years ago, the typical pattern in the islands was that of a wide dispersion of population over the countryside, with the majority of the people engaged directly or indirectly in agriculture and living on their holdings or in small villages and towns often strung out along the roads. The best lands were usually in plantations, and when the slaves were freed, they had to take to the foothills to carve out for themselves small patches of land where they could build a cabin and raise subsistence crops for their own consumption: hence the thousands of tiny houses one sees scattered across the countryside of any West Indian island. In some cases the slaves would be allotted land near the plantation, as the planter still required their labour. So it was that the typical linear village grew up along the road, often with no obvious centre: in Barbados these villages are called 'tenantries'. A village green is a rarity in the West Indies. If there is a focal point it is usually the church (often the only stone building in the village), or perhaps a new government school or clinic. The towns were generally small and mainly centres for trade and administration. There were virtually no factory-based industries, except the sugar refineries (located in the cane-growing areas) and the rum distilleries.

Since World War II a remarkable change has taken place. San Juan, Kingston, Port au Prince, Santo Domingo and Port of Spain have all been transformed from sleepy little towns into bustling metropolitan cities. The larger they become the faster they grow, drawing people irresistibly from the rural areas. Houses cannot be built quickly enough, and still the people come. Often they build themselves a temporary shanty, or they take some substandard accommodation, in the confident hope that they will get a job and then move to something better, or that perhaps the government will rehouse them. In many cases they have to wait for years for the job and the better house, but once they have migrated to the city there is no turning back: they cannot return to the rural areas for there are no jobs for them there either, and no prospects. As the cities grow they acquire more of the symbols of urban civilisation—more neon lights, cinemas, drinking clubs, betting shops and the like. There are also numerous opportunities for earning a little cash in all kinds of casual employment, while any new factories that are established seem always to be located in or near the capital city. The city slum is a staging post, in the minds of its inhabitants, to something better—a necessary rung on the ladder to a decent life; and in the better endowed islands (not Haiti, one hastens to add), a surprising number of the immigrants seem to make good, although this may not be immediately obvious as there are always fresh waves of immigrants following on the heels of those who have moved on and the vacated shanties are quickly reoccupied.

The process just described took San Juan from a town of 70,707 people in 1920 (5·4 per cent of the population) to 589,104 in 1960 (25·1 per cent), and to over 800,000 today (about 30 per cent): it took Santo Domingo from a small and mostly unpaved town of some 32,000 people in the early 1930s to a modern city of over 400,000 people today, and still the inward migration from the rural districts continues at the rate of 25,000 people per annum. It took Port au Prince in a few decades from little more than an overgrown village to a city of 250,000 people, and Kingston from a mere appendage of Spanish Town to a thriving metropolis of over 500,000 inhabitants. Most remarkable of all has been the urbanisation of Trinidad, where 40 per cent of the population now live in the two cities of Port of Spain and San Fernando. Indeed it is a feature of each of these metropolitan centres in the West Indies that they are several times larger than the next largest city in the island.

Some of the cities have grown so fast that they seem more like some vast new housing estate than a capital city. Kingston, Jamaica for instance has very few tall blocks and no obvious city centre. People argue as to whether the city centre is around King Street or in the newly developing area of New Kingston. Now a vast new town is being built at Port-more on the western side of the city to accommodate up to

50,000 people, mainly for the middle classes. San Juan, as befits one of the oldest settlements in the Caribbean, has a well-established city feel about it and a stronger metropolitan atmosphere than any other West Indian city. Half the population of Puerto Rico are now urban dwellers. The French Antilles also have towns with a more marked metropolitan air than is found in most other islands of similar size, thanks largely to the modern high-rise buildings, and no doubt to the French flair for urban living. With their gendarmes, their advertisements for Gauloises, their gourmets and cafés, and their street names in blue and white enamel, these towns have a decidedly Parisian flavour about them. Every town and village has its *mairie,* and its War Memorial to those who died for *la Patrie.*

Often the cities in the Caribbean have evolved a sophisticated way of life that is in marked contrast from that found elsewhere on the island. Perhaps the most obvious example of this is Santo Domingo which became a smart modern city during the Trujillo period and has a sophistication contrasting sharply with the relative poverty of the country areas. Here, as in most of the cities of the West Indies, an altogether disproportionate amount of investment, public and private, has gone into the capital city, leaving the smaller towns and villages often starved of capital for development. Frequently villages are shabby, down at heel and losing population. There are a few examples of new towns designed to draw development away from the capital, like Duvalierville in Haiti, the only one of a number of such developments in Haiti to get off the drawing-board, but on the whole the supremacy of the capital remains unchallenged. Nowhere in the world has the primacy of the capital city become so firmly established as in the West Indies.

Only in the last few years have any effective steps been taken to stem the drift to the cities. In Puerto Rico serious efforts are now being made to deflect new industries from San Juan and special tax exemptions have been introduced to encourage them to move to the provinces: rural services such as roads and telephones are also being improved with the same objective. Other Caribbean countries must surely follow suit soon if the quality of life in the metropolitan centres is to be preserved.

FOOD

The typical West Indian diet is starchy in character, and includes such locally produced foods as yams, rice, okra, sweet potatoes, breadfruit, cassava and maize. Green vegetables are not used very often except in soups, and curiously enough fruit is not an important part of the diet, the main fruits eaten being mangoes, oranges and bananas, although one can hardly ever see bananas for sale in the shops and it is often difficult to obtain this fruit in a hotel. Imported tinned foods seem to be regarded more highly by the housewife than locally grown fresh food and, as shown earlier, the import bill for food is heavy in all the island budgets. Spices are widely used to enliven what might otherwise be a rather dull diet.

The main deficiency in the diet is protein. In particular, meat and livestock products are scarce and, together with fresh milk, are often imported. Barbados for example imports 70 per cent of its milk requirements and most of its beef and mutton—hence the vital importance of the current experiments being conducted to find ways of using sugar-cane as a source of animal feed for cattle. Pork is an important meat and is produced in most of the islands (often pigs are fed on a ration of waste bananas and they seem to thrive on it), while chickens are commonly kept on the smaller farms, mostly running about freely. To supplement their protein sources the West Indians eat a great deal of fish and are among the leading fish eaters in the world. Much of the fish is caught in the seas around their own shores but a substantial proportion is imported from Europe as dried fish, especially dried cod from Norway. The flavour of the salted fish is often preferred to the fresh product and of course it keeps better in the hot climate. Jamaica imports considerable quantities of mackerel from Ireland in plastic barrels, but her main sources of supply are Holland, Norway and Canada. In addition there is still a great deal of local fishing. The housewives surround the fishermen when they haul their boats up on to the beach and the animated bargaining that goes on is one of the most characteristic of Caribbean scenes. Shellfish are very popular and shrimps, crabs and lobsters are found everywhere in the Caribbean oysters are renowned in Haiti. On the Caymans turtles were once caught naturally, but now they are bred on the large turtle-farm, 'Mariculture' on Salt Creek, the only one of its kind in the world.

Although rice is a popular staple food throughout the West Indies, it is noteworthy that it is not grown on many islands. Even Trinidad, where the East Indians are big rice eaters and the conditions are right for growing rice, does not grow enough to meet domestic needs and has to import heavily from Guyana which is indeed the principal source of supply for many West Indian islands. It was the East Indians of Trinidad who introduced wet rice, rather than dry upland rice, into the West Indies. Curry is a popular dish in Trinidad and the curries there are very hot. Another popular dish is roti which is rather like a pancake filled with meat of various kinds. A delicacy of Dominica is 'mountain chicken' or frogs' legs.

The same range of beverages is consumed in the West Indies as in most other countries. Delicious coffee is grown in Jamaica (Blue Mountain coffee) and in Haiti, and cocoa is grown in several islands. Coffee, cocoa and tea are the principal beverages, but since World War II bottled drinks— Coca-cola, Fanta, Seven Up and the like—have become tremendously popular and are now part and parcel of the way of life in the islands. Even the poorest people buy bottled drinks despite their low nutritional value. The weekly trip in the car to return the crate of empties and pick up a fresh one is part of the domestic routine in all the more affluent homes. Among the stronger drinks rum—or *rhum* to use the French word—is still the most common liquor consumed, often mixed with Coca-cola. The light-bodied rums like Bacardi, made in Puerto Rico, the Bahamas and other islands, are becoming more popular than the heavier 'navy' rums. However, imported liquors, especially Scotch whisky, have a status usually higher than that of rum. A unique product of Trinidad is Angostura bitters which is made to a secret formula, details of which are kept locked in a vault in a bank in New York. Another unique West Indian product is the liqueur Tia Maria, made in Jamaica and said to be derived from Blue Mountain coffee-beans.

Everywhere in the West Indies the suburban shopping centre or 'plaza' and the modern supermarket are fast becoming the main form of shopping—at least in the towns. There are many large supermarkets, but some still retain something of the atmosphere of the old grocery store: in Trinidad miscellaneous items are advertised 'wanted or for sale' on a notice-board in the supermarket.

Eating out is becoming as popular in the West Indies as it is elsewhere, but prices tend to be high, and a high proportion of the customers are tourists. Drinking clubs or rum shops are frequented more commonly by the lower-income groups and there are a great number of them in all the islands. Many small sugar or banana farmers dissipate most of their earnings in the rum shops.

Inflation has not had much effect on food prices until recently, and inflation rates were kept down to about 2 per cent or 3 per cent until the last two years. In 1972 the rate of inflation in most of the islands rose suddenly to about 8 per cent, and prices increased sharply. This led some island governments to impose restrictions on price increases in an attempt to stem inflationary increases in the cost of living, but the result was often to cause shortages and even higher rises in prices.

Water

The lack of adequate supplies of drinking water has been
one of the main problems of some of the flatter and drier
islands, particularly Antigua, the Bahamas and the Netherlands Antilles. All these islands now have desalination plants.
During a dry spell in Antigua one is liable to receive a
warning from the authorities that the water may taste a little
salty! Until the Potworks reservoir was completed, with
British aid, there was such a serious shortage of water that
often supplies to the hotels were cut off for days at a time;
naturally, the guests objected, and so the development of
tourism was impeded.

In most of the islands, however, there are hills and mountains and often the problem is not a shortage of water but
too much. Streams and rivers abound and the people often
take their water direct from these in the country areas,
although in the towns stand-pipes or taps in individual houses
are now the rule. Port au Prince still has a water system linked
mainly to stand-pipes and the streets are never empty of
people, often young girls, carrying containers of water on
their heads. It may do wonders for their posture, but it is
heavy and deadly monotonous work and hardly encourages
the family to use the 50-75gal a day that are common in the
developed countries! However, the future may be brighter
for the younger members of Haitian families as the Inter-
American Bank in 1973 voted a loan of US $5.1 million
(about £2 million) to enable the city's water-supplies to be
improved. In the rural areas of many West Indian islands,
however, piped water is still the exception and most homes
depend upon roof catchments, wells or, as mentioned above,
the nearby streams. A survey in 1971 showed that in Haiti
only 3 per cent of rural dwellers had a piped water-supply;
in the Dominican Republic the percentage was 15, in Jamaica
51 and in Trinidad and Tobago 95. The 1970 Census in
Barbados showed that of the 59,266 households, 20,846 had

public piped water into the house, 21,900 depended upon public stand-pipes and 12,304 had public piped water-supply into their yard: the rest depended upon private supplies, roof catchments and other sources.

Sewerage

Until recently, flush toilets and a public sewerage system were the exception rather than the rule in the West Indies, but since World War II modern sewerage systems have been installed in all the larger islands. Trinidad for example has one of the most up-to-date sewerage systems in the world which is designed to serve 500,000 people. In Barbados the 1970 Census showed that of the 59,266 households, 42,065 had pit latrines, while 15,748 had WCs linked to septic tanks. A survey of Haiti in 1971 showed that only 2 per cent of the households had an adequate sewerage system, compared with 7 per cent in the Dominican Republic and 8 per cent in Jamaica. The provision of an adequate supply of domestic water, and proper sewerage, was considered to have a very high priority in the recently published Jamaican Development Plan.

Refuse disposal

In many beautiful West Indian islands the rubbish lying around everywhere is a disgrace and proper refuse disposal services are needed urgently. Yet even where the refuse is removed from the streets, it is sometimes deposited in places where it causes almost as much offence, for example in Dominica, where the refuse from Roseau the capital is deposited near the sea-shore just north of the town, polluting a wide area and making swimming unsafe.

Electricity and gas

The West Indian islands generally have adequate electricity supplies, and most houses and streets in the towns are lit by electricity. In Barbados for example there are 40,000 connections and all but the more remote homes are connected. There are relatively few electrical appliances in use as yet and the power is used mainly for lighting. Only the smallest islands are still without electricity, and one of these, Anguilla, will have its own electricity supplies shortly.

Sources of energy for electricity are varied. In some islands hydroelectric power is harnessed, and the new £12 million (about US $30 million) Peligre Dam in Haiti for instance has gone a long way towards relieving that island's acute shortage. Dominica and Jamaica are among the islands which depend heavily on hydroelectric power. However, the most usual source of energy is thermal power based on steam or diesel. In Puerto Rico 97 per cent of the electricity produced is thermal. In Jamaica, of the fourteen power-stations six are diesel, three are steam and five are hydro. In the Netherlands Antilles electricity is expensive at present, but it is expected that plentiful supplies will become available shortly as a by-product of the expansion of the Lago refinery in Aruba. Puerto Rico used to have a small nuclear-power plant operated experimentally by the Federal Atomic Energy Commission but it is no longer active.

Gas is not widely used as a source of power except in Trinidad and Barbados, where local supplies of natural gas are available.

Health and medical services

Until the present century, the West Indies were almost synonymous with disease and ill-health. People living in the area generally developed some immunity to the diseases such as yellow fever, dysentery, malaria, goitre and yaws. But visitors frequently succumbed after a short time, and it is said that more British troops died of disease on the West Indies station during the Napoleonic Wars than were killed in action in the Peninsular War. However, the discoveries of Ross soon brought about the eradication of malaria, and yellow fever had also been conquered by the turn of the century. By the end of World War II the main diseases still prevalent had become those associated with malnutrition and lack of hygiene, such as gastro-enteritis. In the more primitive districts disease was still endemic, and that remains the situation in Haiti for instance, where the life expectancy is little more than 42 years compared with over 70 in the USA, but elsewhere standards of health are generally on a par with those in Europe or the USA. The life expectancy in Puerto Rico was only 46 years in 1948, but today it is said to be even higher than that of the USA, and this is a typical experience of other West Indian islands.

None of the West Indian islands operates a completely free national health service like that in Britain, but in some of the British Commonwealth islands considerable advances have been made in recent years in that direction. Trinidad and Tobago has a National Health Plan and now has over 100 health centres giving free medical services. In Puerto Rico the pattern is rather more like that in the USA, with medical care being very expensive but the costs being mitigated for many people through membership of the Blue Cross and other medical associations which offer schemes of medical assistance based on low monthly payments. The Government also operates free medical and dental care programmes. In most islands the private health services and those operated by the State exist side by side.

Puerto Rico has an excellent medical service with one doctor per 1,040 people, and one hospital bed per 220 people (in Europe the comparable figures are 640 and 110). Jamaica has one doctor per 1,820 people and one hospital bed per 600 people. Haiti as usual brings up the rear with only one doctor per 17,000 people and one hospital bed per 1,370 people: there are in fact more Haitian doctors working in the USA than in Haiti itself. Most of the islands fall somewhere in this range, with the Bahamas, Netherlands Antilles, Barbados and Trinidad towards the upper end, and the Windward and Leeward Islands and the Dominican Republic towards the

E

lower end. In the smaller islands the building of a single hospital can change the situation drastically: the building of the fine Queen Elizabeth Hospital (583 beds) for instance in Bridgetown, Barbados in the 1950s gave that island one of the best hospitals at that time in the Caribbean. St Vincent hopes to have a new 400-bed hospital soon, and other new hospitals are planned. In the Bahamas a flying doctor service operates to the outlying islands.

Paradoxically, although there is a large number of West Indian doctors and nurses serving abroad, particularly in Britain, one of the main problems in improving the medical services in the West Indies is the shortage of trained staff. Many young medical trainees stay abroad after completing their training because the salaries are higher, or on their return take up private practice because this is more profitable.

National insurance

Until the last decade or so, most of the West Indian islands were too poor to consider national insurance schemes, although some of them had contributory schemes which covered only a small proportion of the population: such a scheme has operated in the Dominican Republic since 1947 and each year a higher percentage of the working population becomes part of it. Trinidad and Tobago instituted an old-age pensions scheme as far back as 1939: it is non-contributory and the benefits are related to age (the qualifying age is sixty-five), number of years' residence (twenty years' minimum to qualify) and a means test (not more than T/T $23 per month). The pension is however very small—from T/T $5 to T/T $18 per month. Public assistance is given to those who cannot earn because of a disability (up to T/T $60 per month for a family).

Jamaica in 1966 introduced a compulsory national insurance scheme modelled on the British system, and in 1967 Barbados followed suit. Contributions are shared between employers and employees. Between June 1967 and August 1971 contributions in Barbados amounted to EC $26 million, and EC $3 million had been paid out in benefits—the balance going towards future pension commitments. Old-age pensioners receive free medical care, help with housing and free travel on buses. In the Bahamas, by way of contrast, there is no national insurance scheme, although the government has introduced an old-age pensions scheme. In the French Antilles the social insurance arrangements are similar to those in metropolitan France and include free medical services and social welfare facilities. In the Netherlands Antilles a law has been passed recently for the setting up of a national insurance scheme.

One of the problems of the smaller and poorer islands is that the people there want a national insurance scheme like the ones existing elsewhere, but these islands are usually too poor to maintain a full health service and they have to settle for something that is but the shadow of the real thing. In Dominica for example the poor relief allowance is EC $1 per week which is a ridiculous sum and almost certainly less than the administrative costs involved. As mentioned earlier, Puerto Rico has no national health scheme: its many private contributory schemes are effective although more expensive. Distressed citizens such as the disabled, the blind and the elderly receive about US $3 per week in cash plus food parcels.

MARRIAGE AND FAMILY LIFE

Marriage

Although generalisations are always dangerous, and nowhere more so than in the West Indies with its polyglot peoples, it can be said that, in general, society in the West Indies tends to be matriarchal, ie it focuses on the mother rather than the father as the centre of the family unit. Marriage as an institution is highly regarded but not always practised: or, to be exact, the wedding ceremony itself is seen usually as the seal or culmination of a marriage that has already proved long-lasting rather than as the beginning of one. The majority of women start their families out of wedlock. In Jamaica for instance 70 per cent of all live births are illegitimate, and in Dominica in 1969 the proportion was 82 per cent. However, the word 'illegitimate' has rather too harsh a ring for the situation as it exists in the West Indies, for many of these women will probably get married later when the husband is able to afford the expense of the wedding ceremony (no mean item in the West Indian budget) and can keep his wife and family at the level which society expects of married people. In the British Commonwealth islands four out of five people are or have been married. During the early years of their partnership most couples live together as man and wife in 'common-law' marriage (sometimes called 'keeper union' or 'faithful concubinage'), and in their own eyes they are as much 'married' as if they had been to church and signed the marriage register. The churches of course are constantly urging couples to get married in church and stress that marriage is a sacrament of the church, in the same way that communion and baptism are, but they have had remarkably little success despite 150 years of trying (marriage was not encouraged during the days of slavery, except in the French territories). Jamaica had a mass marriage campaign in the 1940s, and other islands have had similar campaigns, but they have failed universally.

Although most common-law marriages are permanent unions, there is no denying that the lack of a legal responsibility on the part of the father, combined with the fact that society seems to applaud sexual virility in the male regardless of the consequences, means that there is a distressing number of children who grow up without having a proper father to help to look after them. Moreover the mother is often very young (in Jamaica 34 per cent of women have had their first child at age nineteen or under), and the father also. This means that the couple usually have very little money and have to go out to work to maintain the family. Invariably it is the grandmother or an elderly neighbour who has to look after the children. A revealing phrase in the West Indies is, 'My mother who fathered me'. The anthropologist Edith Clarke has studied family relationships of Jamaicans in great detail and has published her findings in a book with this as the title (based on a phrase which first appeared in George Lamming's *In the Castle of My Skin*) *My Mother Who Fathered Me* (1966). In it she examines the two principal features of family organisation in Jamaica, concubinage as a substitute for marriage among the poorer people, and the high rate of illegitimacy. She also examines the role of the father in the family and finds that although there were a few cases where the father helped to bring up the children with love and care 'it has to be said that examples of paternal devotion and kindness were far outweighed by the cases where he was either no more than the man "who had only fathered the idea of me and left me the sole liability of my mother who really fathered me", or someone remembered for neglect or harsh discipline'.

It is a remarkable fact, attested by surveys, that although the young babies make excellent progress up to the age of one year while they are still at the breast (at that age two or three months in advance of babies in Britain), they fall dramatically behind in their development during the ensuing years so that by the age of four they are estimated to be a year behind the typical British child in language development and in other ways. This is because of the sad lack of mental stimulus in the home: the mother goes out to work and is too tired in the evenings to play with the children; there are few toys in any case, and for most of the day the toddler is left in the 'yard' in the care of an elderly woman. While the child is breast-fed, it will thrive physically, but once it is weaned on to the typical diet of cornmeal porridge with a little condensed milk it will soon show symptoms of undernourishment. Expensive proprietary foods are often advertised in the press and on the radio, but these are usually beyond the means of the poorer families: meanwhile the mother often overlooks the availability of cheaper nutritious foods. Education in child nutrition is thus one of the urgent priorities in social welfare. Malnutrition, vomiting and diarrhoea are still the major causes of disease and death among children of under two years of age.

Family life

The tradition of late marriage (if at all) may lead one to infer that family life in the West Indies is of less importance than elsewhere. But this is not the case. In fact the opposite is true. There is a very strong family life throughout the West Indies and it extends not only to the immediate relatives but to the fourth or fifth cousins as well. It expresses itself for instance in the tradition of caring for the old people in the family no matter how straitened the family circumstances may be. You never see old people's homes in the West Indies, simply because there is no need for them. Someone in the family will always make room for the old folk. Of course in the small wooden shacks of rural Barbados or of Haiti this may increase the problem of overcrowding, but in a warm tropical climate this is less serious than it would be in a temperate climate. It is in keeping with this tradition of family life that divorce is rare. Indeed some of the islands have only recently got round to introducing divorce bills for the first time (St Vincent in 1972 for instance)—particularly those with a strong Roman Catholic background. On the other hand the family tie does not signify an active and corporate family life in the sense that the whole family does things together. It is more a matter of recognising a chain of responsibility in the family rather than a sharing of interests and activities. Husband and wife seldom go out together socially or invite other people to their home, and social gatherings are usually divided by sex: the husband to his club and the wife to her women's gathering. The strongest personal ties within the family are often between a mother and her son and, as a generalisation, the tie between parents and children is usually stronger than that between the parents themselves. Children are still regarded universally in the West Indies as a blessing and a support for old age.

No one can visit the West Indies without being favourably impressed by the appearance of the children. The school-children are always smartly dressed in their school uniform no matter how poor their parents or how depressed the district in which they live, and they always have a ready smile and a sense of fun as all children have. Hitherto there have not been many organised activities for children, but in recent years efforts have been made to provide more creative outlets for them. In Jamaica the 4H clubs (equivalent to the Young Farmers' Clubs in Britain) were started in the 1940s, probably one of the most successful imports from the USA, and today the island has 23,000 members. The 4H movement is mainly rural-based and aims to develop in young people a love of the land, a desire to be efficient agriculturalists and home-makers, and an interest in their own development as young citizens. If it is true that the future of a country lies in its young people, the West Indies are indeed fortunate.

4

How They Work

BEFORE World War II the economies of all the West Indian islands were very depressed. There were too many people for too few jobs. Even before World War I at least 100,000 West Indians emigrated in large numbers to the USA, to Central America or to Cuba. Many Puerto Ricans fled their country, exchanging what was often called 'the Tropical Slum' for slums of another sort in New York: during World War II this flow became a flood and during the seven years from 1944 to 1951 about 250,000 Puerto Ricans emigrated to New York. Making a virtue of necessity, the West Indians simply muttered, 'If crab no walk he no see nothing': they might have added, 'and he no live'.

After World War II there was still widespread unemployment, but more so in the British West Indies than in Puerto Rico, where emigration reached its peak of 75,000 in 1953 and then tailed off rapidly as the economy began to expand. Elsewhere emigration continued at a high rate, but now it was Europe, and particularly Britain, that began to receive the immigrants. The rate of emigration reached its height in 1961 when 60,000 Jamaicans came to Britain. Today it is estimated that there are about 500,000 West Indians living in Britain. The Immigration Acts of 1962 and 1965 in Britain virtually closed the door to substantial West Indian immigration. At the same time Puerto Rico's industrial expansion was getting under way and the new prosperity began to stimulate a return flow back to Puerto Rico: by now there is a rough balance

76

between the numbers of those leaving the country and those entering.

Unhappily Puerto Rico is the exception rather than the rule. In most of the British Commonwealth islands, and in Haiti and the Dominican Republic, unemployment remained at a high level. There has been some migration between the islands (half the labour force in the American Virgin Islands for instance comes from other islands, mainly British West Indians, while in the Bahamas there are 15,000 Haitian workers who entered illegally, usually swimming ashore at night from schooners), but most of the islands have taken steps to prevent these movements by introducing work permits. Normally only certain classes of skilled workers can obtain these permits, and it is these workers who are in short supply in all the West Indian islands, so they have no difficulty in any case in finding jobs. Only France and the Netherlands continued to keep an open door to West Indians, and as their West Indian islands are integral parts of the European countries, it is difficult for them to close this door without also infringing the principle of integral development. The emigration to France has been such that for a number of years the population of Martinique and Guadeloupe actually declined! With the advent of cheap fares to Europe the incidence of emigration is likely to increase, unless restrictions are imposed. Some 10,000 people emigrate from the Netherlands Antilles to the Netherlands each year in search of jobs, but there are signs that the Netherlands Government may not be prepared to let this continue indefinitely. The USA still allows some immigration and in 1971 for instance another 10,000 Haitians joined the 150,000 of their compatriots already in the USA, while in 1969 16,947 Jamaicans emigrated to the USA and 3,889 to Canada. These are valuable outlets but they do not make up for the virtual closing of the door to Britain. The safety-valve of emigration is not yet shut but it is closing, and this has led to an unemployment problem of massive proportions. Unemployment has now become the most important problem in the West Indies.

THE PROBLEM OF UNEMPLOYMENT

In many of the West Indian islands the unemployment rate is now over 20 per cent of the population employed or seeking employment. The Dominican Republic has about 25 per cent unemployed, and in Haiti the rate may be as high as 40 per cent or 50 per cent—no one really knows. Wherever you go there people thrust themselves upon you as guides, following you about the streets until at last you capitulate; taxi-drivers try to book journeys days ahead to be sure of a fare; and many people offer their blood for sale to American blood banks, a flourishing business at present. In Jamaica the unemployment rate is about 15 per cent to 20 per cent and a most disturbing feature is that the majority of unemployed are young men aged under twenty-five: they number about 100,000 compared with the total labour force of some 750,000. For many young Jamaicans 'scuffling' or wandering around trying to pick up some odd job that may be going, has now become a way of life. Youth camps and youth welfare and training establishments are being set up all over Jamaica, but they will cater for only about 20,000 by 1975; and bearing in mind that each year another 33,000 young Jamaicans are looking for jobs, the employment situation must surely get worse rather than better. In Trinidad the unemployment rate is about 15 per cent and in 1970 the Government introduced a tax called an Unemployment Levy, to enable it to undertake emergency public works as unemployment relief. Even in the Netherlands Antilles, where the standard of living is relatively high on account of the oil industry, unemployment is up to about 20 per cent. As a result of improved techniques and widespread mechanisation, employment in the oil industry fell from 20,000 in the 1950s to about 4,500 today. Even in Puerto Rico, with its booming economy, there is an unemployment rate of 10 per cent.

One of the great paradoxes of the West Indian employment

situation is that although unemployment is severe in so many of the islands there are some jobs which people dislike so much that they often refuse to do them even if the alternative is unemployment and hardship. The main example is that of cutting sugar-cane. This is a back-breaking and dirty job that has to be done in the broiling sun, and it is associated in people's minds with slavery. In Jamaica, Trinidad and Barbados, indeed everywhere in the West Indies, cane-cutting is heartily disliked and often the job has to be done by people from other islands who seem less concerned about the social stigma involved when they are away from their own people. Each year some 1,200 St Vincentians move across to Barbados to cut sugar-cane despite the unemployment on that island, and 40 per cent of the cane-cutters in the Dominican Republic come from Haiti. This resistance to cane-cutting is becoming more and more a reluctance to do manual agricultural work in general. In Trinidad the drift to the cities in search of work in the booming economy has led to a severe dearth of workers in the rural areas: sugar-cane is not cut, limes are left on the trees unpicked and the coconuts are sometimes left to rot. To understand this aversion to hard, manual, agricultural work, one has to remember that the West Indian small farmer does not spring from an indigenous peasantry: his forebears were slaves or indentured workers, hence Sidney Muntz's accurate description of the West Indian farmers as a 'rural proletariat'.

Another significant feature of the West Indian employment situation is the existence of a severe shortage of skilled workers alongside a surplus of unskilled workers. In Trinidad, as in most of the islands, masons, carpenters and craftsmen of all kinds are in short supply. One of the problems is that as soon as a West Indian learns a trade or a skill he quickly discovers that he can earn double or treble his pay in the West Indies by emigrating to the USA or elsewhere, and as he is a skilled worker he is likely to obtain an entry permit. Hence there is a continual drain on the resources of skilled labour in the region.

ROLE OF THE TRADE UNIONS

Trade union activity began in the West Indies during the labour troubles of the 1930s. In Trinidad, where the unions are stronger than in most of the other islands, the first union was established in 1934 and today there are eleven unions with 50,000 members affiliated to the Trinidad and Tobago Labour Congress, and another three unions not affiliated. There is strong interunion rivalry between the Trades Union Congress and the National Federation of Labour. The strike situation in Trinidad became very bad during the 1960s and the demands of the unions became ever more extreme, with claims for wage increases of up to 75 per cent and demands for full pay for strikers. The situation deteriorated so much that the government introduced a number of measures aimed at more sophisticated negotiation and arbitration procedures, and these culminated in 1972 in the Industrial Relations Bill which attempts to restrain the worst excesses of trade union activity. Sir Arthur Lewis in his speech to the second Annual General Meeting of the Caribbean Development Bank, in 1972, stressed the need of the West Indian islands for an effective incomes policy.

Interunion rivalry is a feature of trade union life in Jamaica also, but in this case each of the two rival unions has strong political affiliations, one supporting the Jamaican Labour Party (Bustamente's Industrial Trade Union), and the other the People's National Party (National Workers Union). The smaller islands, such as the Bahamas (sixteen trade unions registered), Antigua and St Lucia (where a Trades Union Council has been launched recently), also have an active trade union life. In Puerto Rico, the big American trade unions made a determined and successful attempt to capture the allegiance of the workers in the island, and as a result they have been instrumental in pushing wages towards the levels prevailing in the USA itself. They have been able to achieve this without massive unemployment only because of the heavy inflow of American capital and the economic expansion

which this has made possible. The Dominican Republic and
Haiti have very little trade union activity, and it is indi-
cative of the weakness of the unions in Haiti that when 200
workers went on strike at an Amercan project there in 1972
they were all promptly sacked and the unions were powerless
to do anything about it.

'MADE IN THE WEST INDIES'—THE GROWTH
OF INDUSTRY

The traditional industries of the West Indies have been
the processing of agricultural and forest products. Disused
sail-less windmills and wheel-less watermills can be seen all
over the Caribbean, the sugar and rum factories of a past age;
and many small processing establishments still exist, such as
bay oil stills in Dominica, tobacco-drying sheds in Jamaica,
banana-boxing plants in the Windwards and copra sheds and
mat-making workshops in numerous other places. The processing of mineral products is another traditional West Indian
industry: salt pans in Anguilla, pumice quarries in Dominica,
cement plants in Jamaica or the small potteries found here
and there throughout the Caribbean.

These small processing industries still characterise the
lesser islands, but in the larger ones factories of the European
or American type are beginning to appear. Around Kingston,
Port of Spain or San Juan, one sees industrial estates springing
up that would not be out of place in Slough or New Jersey.
As yet there is little heavy industry, but all the smaller items
such as clothing, food, furniture and miscellaneous goods of
all kinds are now made in the West Indies.

The West Indian islands lack most of the requirements for
rapid industrial development: their domestic markets are
generally small, purchasing power is often low, there is a
shortage of coal or iron ore for heavy industry, and the frag-
mentation into small islands leads to difficult problems of
transport and marketing. The heavy dependence of the islands

on export crops means that ships coming out to load with bananas, sugar or citrus fruits, often have spare capacity on the outward journey so that freight costs on imported manufactured goods are less than they would otherwise be.

However, there is one resource on the islands which is becoming scarcer all the time in the developed countries, and that is an abundant supply of relatively cheap, if unskilled, labour. It is this resource which has attracted industry on a large scale since the end of World War II. The process began with the remarkable success of the Puerto Rican 'Operation Bootstrap', a policy of encouragement to all kinds of industrial development which has brought some 200 new factories to Puerto Rico. The island's industrial sector has grown by 12·5 per cent per annum since 1940 and now represents one-quarter of the total national income. Puerto Rico today ranks fifth among the USA's overseas markets. Nor is Puerto Rico resting on its laurels: in 1971 plans were announced for a further US $4 billion of industrial investment by 1980. Net income per head is expected to be £800 (about US $2,000) per annum by 1975. From poverty to relative affluence in one generation—this is indeed a remarkable achievement.

The industries that were attracted to Puerto Rico, especially in the early days, were typically those requiring a great deal of unskilled labour, such as textiles, needlework, handicrafts, leather goods, hats, furniture, hosiery, novelties, artificial flowers and the like. Taking their cue, the other islands have set out to copy Puerto Rico and have also been able to attract new industries of this type. The Dominican Republic and Haiti, for example, with their very low wage levels, have attracted many American firms in the last few years as wages continue to rise in Puerto Rico. In Haiti's mini-boom since the death of 'Papa Doc', 150 light industries employing some 10,000 people have been established and there is now a growing flood of baseball gloves, jeans, underwear, electrical goods and other such labour-intensive products, exported from Haiti to the USA. Often the degree of skill needed in these new industries is marginal, as in the blank sock industry of Trinidad which simply involves putting the toe into socks already half-finished by machine; or the watch assembly industry which involves merely the assembling of parts manufactured elsewhere. Mr Manley, Prime Minister of Jamaica, christened them 'screwdriver industries'. Frequently they are criticised on the grounds that they bring little permanent benefit to the islands in the form of skills learned or even financial profits, since the 'value added' in the operations conducted in the West Indies is usually minimal, especially if one takes into account the substantial tax concessions that are often offered to attract these industries in the first place. The debate still rages as to whether this kind of industry is of much benefit to the West Indies, but the fact remains that it was the ladder by which Puerto Rico climbed out of its rut and if one country can do it, why not others?

There is a marked hierarchy of incomes in most West Indian islands, with a relatively small section of the population who happen to be in the highly capital-intensive and often foreign-owned industries like bauxite and oil, earning incomes several times higher than those in the labour-intensive industries or in agriculture. In Trinidad the capital invested per man employed in the oil industry is EC $76,000 whereas in agriculture it cannot be more than a few thousand dollars. The statistics for Trinidad reflect the hierarchy of incomes:

Average wages bill per employee in Trinidad (1971)

T/T $ per annum

Oil	5,000 (ie about £1,000 or US $2,500)
Drink and tobacco	2,800
Food manufacture	2,200
Textiles, footwear and wearing apparel	1,100

Statistics for Jamaica show that salaries in the bauxite and alumina industry are about double those elsewhere.

At the upper end of the scale are the civil servants who have had substantial wage increases in recent years. In Trinidad and Tobago top civil servants earn T/T $25,000 per annum. At the bottom end of the scale are the large numbers of people who continue to make a living selling miscellaneous items of small value in the street markets. One sees them in downtown Port of Spain, Kingston or Port au Prince, indeed almost anywhere in the West Indies. It is a permanent mystery how they survive. Only slightly better off are the plantation workers and small farmers, and the unskilled manual workers who work on building sites or as cleaners and waiters. There tends to be only a small middle-class community in most of the islands, except in Puerto Rico where the great variety of industrial jobs has led to the emergence in recent years of a large middle class; the same process is beginning in Jamaica also. The trends since World War II have been towards a continual decline in agriculture and a gradual increase in industrial employment, tourism, the service industries and the civil service. Thanks to the power of the trade unions in the better organised industries, wages in the industrial sector

———————

Unloading sugar-cane at a factory in Jamaica

Carrying bananas in the old market, Roseau, Dominica

have been rising rapidly, and although only a decade ago wages in the West Indies were very low compared with those in the USA (in Trinidad for instance only about one-fifth), the differential is now very much less except in Haiti and the Dominican Republic. While this is of course to be welcomed in one respect, it undoubtedly diminishes the advantages of the region to potential industrialists.

Several West Indian countries now operate minimum wage legislation. Trinidad and the Netherlands Antilles introduced such a scheme early in 1973, and even Haiti raised its minimum wage from 60 cents per day to $1 in 1972. Jamaica has legislation ·dealing with holidays with pay, covering all employees except those in local and national government (who have their own arrangements) and Trinidad also has a Terms of Employment Bill under discussion.

THE JOBS PEOPLE DO

The sugar industry

Sugar-cane and slavery have always been linked. The one was made possible by the other, and sugar has borne the

Experimental cableway for bananas in St Lucia

Loading bananas for the Geest boat, Portsmouth, Dominica

F

taint of slavery ever since, even long after emancipation. Sugar is produced both on large plantations (pre-empting the flatter coastal lands) and by smallholders, usually occupying the poorer land in the foothills and mountains. At one extreme is the 95,000-acre estate (70,000 acres of it in sugar-cane) of Rio Haina in the Dominican Republic and at the other are the miniscule holdings of Nevis where each grower has only an acre or two of cane. Most islands have examples of both, and the contrast between them constitutes the 'dual economy' that is so characteristic of the West Indies. On the one hand are the large, well-run, foreign-owned plantations producing crops mainly for export, and on the other are tens of thousands of small farmers, tradespeople, hucksters and higglers, who operate on a tiny scale and earn barely enough to keep themselves alive. The statistics of land distribution tell the story. In Grenada, a typical example, there are 12,510 holdings with less than 5 acres each, which account for only 23·9 per cent of the total acreage, while there are only 92 holdings with over 100 acres each, but these account for 46 per cent of the acreage.

Cutting sugar-cane is a dirty job, as mentioned earlier, because the canes are usually burnt as they stand in the fields a few hours before cutting begins. This is done to burn away the leaves and other 'trash', so that the workers can cut more sugar-cane per hour—they are paid on the quantity of cane they cut. Sometimes people set fire to the cane before the cutters are ready to cut it (the sugar content falls if the cane is not cut within a few hours of burning) and these are called 'malicious fires': about one-quarter of Trinidad's cane crop was damaged in this way in 1973. The cut canes are taken to the sugar factories where the juice is extracted and turned into raw sugar for export mainly to Europe or North America where it is further refined into white sugar. During the cutting season, which lasts from January to May, the roads are choked with lorries piled high with cane, either stacked neatly by hand or heaped higgledy-piggledy after having been loaded by mechanical grab. At the factory, chains are passed under each load and the whole contents are lifted from the lorry in one operation and deposited on the mountain of cane waiting to enter the factory. Employment in the sugar factories provides an important industrial sector in some islands which otherwise would have little or no industry.

The banana industry

This industry is a close runner-up to sugar as the most characteristic of West Indian industries. Bananas are ideally suited to peasant agriculture, and there are several hundred thousand small growers dependent on the industry in the West Indies. There is no taint of slavery and indeed the Windward Islands have an enviable reputation for political stability because of their peasant-based agricultures. Most of the growers own only a few acres in the more hilly areas, often some distance from their homes, so that they have to walk up to the banana fields every day, or hope to get a lift in a lorry. The fertilisers are supplied by the Banana Growers Associations who also do the spraying—from the air, as a rule. The most arduous work is 'heading' the heavy stems of bananas to the lorry for the journey to the boxing plant. All too often one sees quite young children who should certainly be in school, doing this work, but usually men are hired for the purpose. The bananas are cut according to a strict schedule which is geared to the arrival of the banana boats. These boats have fixed sailings every week and sufficient quantities of bananas have to be cut and carried to the quayside to ensure that the ships can be loaded as quickly as possible. Watching the long lines of women carrying the banana boxes on their heads from the storesheds to the lighter, half running so that they maximise their earnings, is one of the unforgettable scenes in the Windward Islands, as is the sight of the sleek white Geest banana ships waiting offshore to receive their cargoes.

There is no processing industry connected with bananas as there is with sugar, but in recent years it has become the practice to pack the hands of bananas into cardboard boxes for safe shipment, and several hundred boxing plants have been built in the Windward Islands and in Jamaica. Quite a number of people find employment in these, selecting the fruit, soaking it in the tanks of fungicide and skilfully packing the hands into the cartons so that they will not jog about and be bruised en route. Unfortunately, the boxing plants operate for only two or three days each week and the employment therefore is spasmodic.

The citrus and coconut industries

These are now so much a part of the Caribbean scene that it comes as something of a surprise to learn that they were started by the Europeans. It was Columbus who introduced citrus, the fruit that had been newly brought to Portugal from the Arab countries. Oranges, limes, tangerines and the new variety, 'ortaniques' (grown in Jamaica, these are a cross between an orange and a tangerine—the 'ique' is just for effect) are the varieties of citrus chiefly grown, together with grapefruit. Jamaica is the principal producer but nearly all the other islands, except the flat dry ones, also grow citrus fruits. One sees few large orange groves like those in Mediterranean countries; instead the citrus trees are grown here and there, often interspersed with other tree crops in the upland areas, and they are generally grown by smallholders rather than on a plantation basis. A substantial part of the crop is sold on the local market, or it is turned into juice or oil for export. The production of lime oil for instance provides employment for some 12,000 people in Jamaica, 5,000 in Trinidad and 1,000 in Dominica where the famous Roses lime-juice firm has been operating for over a century.

Coconuts are found growing on most of the West Indian islands, particularly along the eastern coasts. The long slender trees with their fine tracery of leaves are a photographer's delight, and no tourist beach is complete without its fringe of coconut trees (although the hotel manager often

takes the wise precaution of having the nuts removed, as
people have been killed by falling nuts). The nuts are cracked
open by the growers and the white fleshy part is dried in the
sun to be sold as copra for manufacture into oil, soap, animal
feeds and a multitude of other products. Coir, the material
from which the traditional coir mattresses found throughout
the West Indies are made, is also obtained from the coconut.

Other agricultural products

Before sugar became king, coffee was the principal crop of
many West Indian islands. It is still grown widely, but on a
small scale, except in Haiti where it is the dominant crop.
Cocoa is another crop that is grown quite widely, mainly in
the Dominican Republic, Jamaica, Trinidad and Grenada.
Sea-island cotton is staging a comeback in demand and
production is being expanded rapidly in Barbados, Antigua
and St Kitts and Nevis. Trials are now being made of
possible cotton-picking machinery. Sisal is grown mainly in
Haiti and in the Bahamas. Tobacco is grown on the majority
of the islands and some of them grow enough for their own
needs. Jamaica has a large cigarette factory (Carreras at
Kingston) and also produces quality cigars. Cereals are seldom
grown on the islands except in the Dominican Republic.
Spices are among the more exotic products of the West Indies.
Some of them are unique to the region, for instance pimento
which is grown only in Jamaica. Ginger also is grown in
Jamaica and is becoming important in other islands such as
St Lucia and Trinidad. Grenada is renowned for its mace
and nutmegs, which have been grown there since the mid-
nineteenth century and have given the island the title of
'Spice Island of the West'. Another crop found widely in the
West Indies is arrowroot, a speciality of St Vincent. The
growing of vegetables has been a surprisingly neglected area
of West Indian agriculture until recently, and one seldom
sees a vegetable patch or 'kitchen garden' attached to a West
Indian house. However, with the rapid development of the

tourism industry in recent years, a new and lucrative market has opened up for good-quality vegetables, and a great deal of research and effort is going into the development of this industry.

The livestock sector is very weak in all West Indian islands, except perhaps in the Dominican Republic where livestock are much more in evidence than elsewhere, but strenuous attempts have been made in recent years to stimulate the growth of a prosperous livestock industry. The West Indians, like people everywhere, are demanding more animal products in their diet, and agriculture must respond if it is to meet the needs of the region.

Forestry and fishing

These two resources have not as yet been fully exploited in most West Indian islands. It is often forgotten that in the Caribbean, with its sun-drenched beaches and eternal summer, there are some of the finest stands of virgin rain forest left in the world. Most of Dominica for instance is rain forest, much of it totally unexploited and even unexplored. In Trinidad, forests cover about half the land area, while the Blue Mountains of Jamaica are clothed with magnificent rain forest. Jamaica has 655,000 acres of forest, ie one-quarter of the total land area. A considerable variety of trees grows in the Caribbean because of the wide climatic range. In the wetter areas, the main varieties include Gommier, Bois Blanc and Balata; in the drier areas such as Haiti and the Bahamas one finds mainly pines. Despite the abundance of timber, however, it is not exploited effectively and instead of the islands being big exporters of timber the reverse is often the case. The problems of gaining access to the more valuable trees in the rain forest areas are indeed formidable and were among the factors that led to the early demise of the recently established timber industry of Dominica. A great deal more capital and expertise will be required before the timber resources of the West Indies can be utilised efficiently.

Fishing is important throughout the Caribbean. It is usually inshore fishing from small boats, often little more than canoes, and great skill and seamanship are required on the dangerous Atlantic coasts of the islands in the Eastern Caribbean. However, domestic supplies account for only about one-third of the fish consumed in the region; the rest is imported. The fact is that fishing has been a declining industry for a long time. Each year there are fewer people who are prepared to endure the hardships, the dangers and the uncertain income attached to inshore fishing in small boats, and increasingly attention is being turned to the possibility of exploiting the fisheries of the deeper waters off the Continental Shelf, using motor trawlers.

From 1966 to 1972 the United Nations ran a Caribbean Fisheries Development Project centred on Bridgetown, Barbados, in which fifteen West Indian countries took part. They have been able to prove that the Caribbean would be able to supply all the region's needs for fish if the industry were modernised and expanded. At present the West Indies needs about 270,000 tons of fish per annum, but by 1980 it will need 400,000 tons. The Trinidad Government has formed a National Fisheries Company to buy ten fishing trawlers to exploit the local reserves. It has also, together with the Barbados and Guyanese Governments, set up the Caribbean Fisheries Training and Development Institute which opened in 1973. Barbados too is increasing its fishing fleet and is buying sixteen modern trawlers. As a result of all these developments, it is expected that some 400 trawlers will be operating eventually in the Continental Shelf area.

Jamaica has begun a major modernisation scheme based on larger deep-sea fishing boats to be built entirely in Jamaica, and as part of this scheme a modern dry-dock costing J $500,000 was opened in 1973. Another part of the Caribbean where fishing is undergoing an expansion is the Bahamas. In 1971 ten ferro-cement boats of an advanced design were built for the fishing fleet and more are planned. In Puerto Rico fish-ponds constructed artificially for the purpose are proving popular, as in the USA itself, and they now cover a surface area of 5,600 acres.

The West Indian fisheries are thus being rapidly modernised and their productive efficiency is much increased. But at the same time, fewer people are likely to be employed as the number of individual fishermen declines gradually. It is most improbable that the fishing industry, any more than agriculture, will make much of a contribution towards solving the employment problem in the West Indies.

THE EXTRACTIVE INDUSTRIES

Bauxite and alumina

The bauxite industry exists on three West Indian islands. It is most important in Jamaica, which was, until Australia overtook it recently, the world's leading exporter of both the raw material bauxite and the alumina derived from it; and it exists also in the Dominican Republic where Alcoa USA mines about 1 million tons of bauxite at Pedernales near the Haitian border, and in Haiti (again mined by an American company) but only on a small scale.

Bauxite mining began in Jamaica in 1952 and today bauxite (with alumina) is the biggest single contributor to the country's national product (20 per cent) and employs some 12,000 people, which is proportionately much fewer than are employed in agriculture, but the wages are very much higher. A National Bauxite Commission was established in 1972 to have general oversight of the affairs of the industry.

The bauxite is mined in about half a dozen locations in the central part of Jamaica, and the bauxite companies own some 200,000 acres of land, which makes them the largest landowners in the country. Much of this land is kept in reserve for future mining and is at present still farmed, so that the bauxite companies are also very important so far as agriculture is concerned. Because the bauxite occurs generally at inland sites, one of the principal problems facing the industry is that of transport to the coast for shipment abroad. As bauxite is a bulky commodity, much of it is sent by road to ports specially built to handle the bauxite carriers on both the north and south coasts of Jamaica. Most of the bauxite goes to the USA, where it supplies about half America's needs; the alumina is exported to Canada and Norway.

Like iron-mining, bauxite extraction does great damage to the landscape and in recent years increasing concern has been expressed on this score, so that it is now compulsory for the mining companies to restore the environment when working ceases.

Alumina is produced in two places in the West Indies where no bauxite exists—Aruba and the American Virgin Islands. The bauxite is all imported here and the smelting into alumina is done using electricity derived from imported oil. In the American Virgin Islands the firm of Harvie Aluminium has a £26 million (about US $65 million) alumina plant alongside the Hess Oil installation erected in 1966, and there are plans for the further expansion of both.

The future of the bauxite industry in the West Indies looks bright, since reserves are extensive and demand is buoyant. The present trend for more of the raw bauxite to be turned into alumina in situ is likely to continue in the years ahead, and Jamaica estimates that its eventual capacity is for 4.5 million tons of alumina (as compared with about 2 million tons now). The main problem in Jamaica is to find a cheap source of abundant power, and plans are now well advanced for a possible alumina plant at Yallahs River in association with a large new oil refinery. Jamaica's fear is that other islands may offer cheap electricity, especially those which have large oil refineries already, and that the alumina industry may expand there rather than in Jamaica. Another possible development is the use of alumina waste for the production of iron titaniumdioxide and liquid alum as the basis for a Jamaican steel industry.

Other minerals

The most important mineral product in the West Indies, after bauxite, is nickel, but it is only very recently that the commercial exploitation of this metal was begun. In 1972 the Canadian firm of Falconbridge opened its large new ferro-nickel metallurgical complex at Benao in the heart of the Dominican Republic. This huge $200 million plant produces about 63 million pounds of ferro-nickel per annum and employs 1,400 people. It is estimated that the reserves will last for twenty years. The Dominican Republic also produces small quantities of iron ore which are exported.

So far as non-metalliferous deposits are concerned, the West Indies yields abundant supplies of most of the usual building materials, including limestone for cement manufacture (very important in view of the tremendous activity in the construction industry since World War II), gypsum (Jamaica is a big exporter), sand, silica, gravel and clay. Other important minerals are phosphates (mined in Curaçao, where the industry employs 350 men, and in Jamaica), marble (fast becoming a popular building material in Jamaica) and salt. Salt is produced in a number of West Indian islands, of which the most important are Aruba (120,000 tons were produced in 1972 and production is forecast to rise to 500,000 tons by 1975); the Bahamas, where the main centre is Great Inagua, producing 250,000 tons and employing 300 men and a dozen vessels; the Turks and Caicos; and tiny Anguilla.

One of the best known mineral resources of the West Indies is asphalt from the Pitch Lake in Trinidad. The Pitch Lake, about 100 acres in extent, has no parallel anywhere in the world. Although extraction has been going on for the greater part of a century, the level of the lake has hardly changed, owing to continuous seepage from the under-lying oil deposits.

The great lack in the West Indies hitherto has been adequate supplies of fuel. There are some very low-grade lignite deposits in the Dominican Republic, but otherwise coal has been totally lacking. Charcoal has been used very much in the past for producing heat in factories, and hydro-electric power has been generated in some islands, but the lack of fossil fuels has undoubtedly inhibited industrial development. Trinidad has been fortunate in finding oil (see below) but so far, despite the most intensive exploration, no oil has yet been discovered in sufficient quantity for commercial use on any other island. In Barbados a well was sunk to 13,488ft before it was abandoned without oil having been struck (natural gas, however, is produced on the island). In Jamaica a number of test bores proved abortive during the 1950s and prospecting stopped for the time being, but it has since been resumed, especially in the south-west of the island. In St Vincent an American company signed an agreement with the government in 1972, obtaining the right to explore for oil in and around St Vincent and the Grenadines. In Grenada the government is investigating its legal position vis-a-vis sea-bed rights to oil, particularly in relation to Trinidad. In Aruba seismic surveys have been started in the waters around the island as part of the oil exploration programme. In the Bahamas the Bahamas Gulf Oil Company is doing intensive drilling in an area half a mile offshore at Clarence Town, Long Island and there seems to be a real prospect of oil being struck. So the search continues with ever increasing intensity—the latter-day search for a new El Dorado.

Oil and natural gas

Oil was being exploited from the vicinity of the Pitch Lake two years before the famous Drake Well was dug in Pennsylvania in 1859. The oil industry in the West Indies has therefore had a long history, but production was never large and in the post-war years it was declining. After 1945 Trinidad's refining capacity exceeded its own production and crude oil had to be imported to help the refineries to keep operating. Then during the 1960s and early 1970s the situation changed dramatically with the discovery of important underwater fields off Trinidad's south-eastern coast. In December 1971 a consortium was set up to launch further oil exploration off the south-east coast, comprising Texaco-Trinidad (37.5 per cent), Shell-Trinidad (37.5 per cent) and Trinidad-Tesoro (25 per cent). Other major oil companies have been exploring also, particularly Amoco-Trinidad and the Natural Gas Pipeline Company of the USA which has begun to work the 'Teak' field some 25 miles off the east coast of Trinidad; from this field a 16ft transmission line has been laid to a 1,600ft jetty at Galeota Point. Amoco also has built a 42ft loading line to a single-point mooring buoy 3 miles offshore which is capable of taking 250,000ton tankers. Texaco has also started commercial production of oil from the new underwater fields and has constructed another single-point mooring installation to accommodate the mammoth tankers. By December 1972 the total production of crude oil was about 200,000 barrels a day and output is still increasing rapidly. There are also ambitious plans for exploiting Trinidad's natural gas resources. Amoco is planning to establish a T/T $400 million liquid natural gas plant to be served by a fleet of specially designed tankers estimated to cost, in all, T/T $300 million. First shipments are scheduled for 1976. These natural gas reserves are expected to last for at least twenty-five years.

Trinidad's economic situation has been completely transformed by these massive discoveries of oil and gas, just at the time when its sugar industry was facing collapse. Now it has one of the fastest rates of economic growth of any Caribbean country. For Trinidad, El Dorado is a reality.

THE PROCESSING INDUSTRIES

Oil refineries and oil transhipment

No other industry has had a more dramatic expansion in the Caribbean in recent years than oil refining. The mainsprings of all this activity have been the rising demand for low-sulphur petroleum in the USA (ie to reduce atmospheric pollution); the inability of American domestic production to meet rising consumption; and the need to import oil in large quantities from the Middle East. In addition the internal demand for petroleum within the larger West Indian islands has risen sufficiently to justify the establishment of refineries.

Taking this latter aspect first, oil refineries have now been constructed in Puerto Rico (at San Juan and at Ponce where there is a large petro-chemical complex), the Dominican Republic, Jamaica and Martinique, to supply domestic requirements. In Jamaica the government and the SARAS group of Italy are investing J $318 million in the Luana oil refinery at St Elizabeth, and construction work is expected to start in 1974. The large Hess oil refinery on the American Virgin Islands, as mentioned earlier, is operated in connection with the production of alumina, and the proposed Yallahs River project in Jamaica, as well as providing energy for alumina production, will also provide petrol for domestic use and for export to the USA. This will be 'clean' (ie low-sulphur) petrol and these refineries are sometimes nicknamed 'laundromat' refineries.

On the refining-for-export side of the industry, the outstanding examples are Curaçao, which has had important refining installations since 1916 (Shell) and Aruba which has had a refinery since 1925. These two refinery complexes are among the largest in the world, and a third has since been built on the smaller island of Bonaire. At first the Netherlands Antilles' lead was unchallenged, but then Trinidad entered the scene. To supplement its domestic supplies it began to import crude oil from Venezuela, and then when the demand from the USA for low-sulphur petrol became dominant it turned to importing the 'very clean' oil from Libya and blending it with the 'dirtier' Venezuelan and Trinidadian oil for sale in the USA. Despite these developments, however, the demand has risen faster than the supply, and in 1970 a large new refinery was established at Freeport in the Bahamas, by the Bahamas Oil Refining Company; this is now the biggest in the world for the manufacture of low-sulphur fuel oils. A petro-chemical industry is already beginning to grow up round this refinery, using naphtha by-products to produce synthetic rubber, plastics, chemicals and detergents. In 1973 the Bahamas Oil Refining Company embarked on a further massive expansion of its refinery which will bring its total investment in the industry there to £68 million (about US $170 million). Another proposal at present under discussion is for an oil refinery at Providenciales in the Turks and Caicos Islands to employ 2,700 people, about equal to the total labour force of these small islands.

A new development in the growth of the West Indies oil industry is the use of the Caribbean as a transhipment point for oil cargoes. The largest modern tankers now coming into use cannot get near enough to the Gulf Ports of the USA, and to much of the eastern seaboard, to discharge their cargoes, and in any case the quantity of oil carried in a 400,000ton tanker is simply too much for one refinery to handle economically. It is therefore both necessary and convenient to split the cargo into smaller lots. The obvious place for this is in the Eastern Caribbean. In 1973 plans were agreed for the establishment at Grand Bahama of a $30 million deep-water petroleum terminal, to accommodate 350,000ton tankers bringing crude oil from the Middle East to be transhipped into smaller tankers of, say, 100,000 tons for onward shipment to ports in the USA. Associated with the plans for a new refinery in the Turks and Caicos is a scheme for another of these transhipment terminals, utilising the deep water a few feet offshore.

One can hardly keep pace with all these large-scale developments. Although they will undoubtedly bring great economic advantages to the region, one cannot help wondering what the effect on the landscape will be, and even more, on the air the West Indians breathe. And what would happen if one of these monster tankers were to hit a reef? Is America buying relief from atmospheric and possibly sea pollution, at the expense of the Caribbean? If so, economic progress may prove to have been dearly bought.

Other processing industries

After oil, the next most important processing industry is alumina, which has been mentioned already, and then cement which has become a major industry on some of the islands. The huge, modern cement works on Grand Bahama for instance produces nearly 1 million tons of cement per annum, using the very pure limestone dredged from Freeport harbour. All the larger islands now have their own cement works, and they supply their smaller neighbours with what one writer has called 'the ubiquitous flow of cement'. Other processing industries include the manufacture of coir mattresses, the use of bagasse (residue of sugar refining) for hardboard panels for building purposes and for animal feeds, furniture making, clay tiles, concrete blocks, cigars, UHT milk (Nestlés has factories in the Dominican Republic and in Trinidad), soap and edible oils (Unilever operate in Trinidad and Jamaica), breweries, citrus juices, flour mills, rum, chocolate, tanneries, handicrafts and so on.

THE MANUFACTURING INDUSTRIES

Light industry is now well established in the West Indies, but as yet heavy industry has hardly started at all, nor is it ever likely to be very important because of the relatively small size of the market. The main industry of this kind is ship-repairing, which owes its existence to the location of the Caribbean athwart the entrance to the Panama Canal where many shipping lines converge. At Curaçao a new dry-dock was completed in 1972, capable of taking ships of 120,000 tons deadweight and costing £9 million (about US $22 million). This is located on the island's west coast. The natural harbour of Willemstad has for centuries been a centre for ship-repairing. The weather in the Caribbean is particularly favourable for outdoor work: fog is unknown and humidity here is low. The dockyard at Curaçao handles about 1,000 ships per annum and on some days more ships dock at Curaçao and Aruba than in New York: these two islands have some of the finest ship-repairing facilities in the western hemisphere. The other important centre for ship-repairing is San Juan, Puerto Rico where there are docks capable of taking ships up to 20,000 tons deadweight.

Very little steel is manufactured yet in the Caribbean, but the industry has made some small beginnings. Jamaica has had a steel mill for a number of years, and in Trinidad a small mill was built in 1971 by Caribbean Steel Mills Limited at Arima. Scrap steel from Trinidad (including the lines from the disused railway) will be sold to Venezuela in exchange for steel billets which will be made up into a variety of steel products such as angles, flats, pipes and reinforcing rods. However, it will probably always be cheaper to import most of the steel required in the West Indies than to attempt to manufacture it locally.

TOURISM

Except in Haiti and the Dominican Republic, where its growth has been stultified by political disturbances, tourism has become one of the major industries in all the West Indian

Mechanical diggers on the Pitch Lake, Port of Spain, Trinidad

Mining bauxite near Mandeville, Jamaica

islands. So rapid has been its rate of growth, however, and it has brought so many social problems in its train, that the tourist industry has caused more heart-searching than any other post-war development in the Caribbean.

The annual rate of growth has been breathtaking, so much so that when it slows from 20 per cent to, say, 5 per cent everyone talks of a severe 'recession' in the industry. In 1971 the Bahamas had 1.46 million visitors compared with a permanent population of only 169,000, and over 1 million tourists visited Puerto Rico. In 1972 480,000 came to Jamaica (87 per cent from North America) and 210,000 to Barbados. Yet only twenty years ago the visitors to these islands were numbered in mere thousands. Grand Bahama had only a few hundred hotel beds in 1963; today it has 4,000. In 1964 St Lucia's tourist receipts were only EC $1.6 million, in 1970 they were EC $6 million, and today they must be over EC $10 million. It is forecast that by 1980 Puerto Rico will have 40,000 hotel beds, and already the Condado Strip and Isla Verde at San Juan challenge Miami Beach for sheer opulence, and far excel it for intelligent use of resources . . . one can actually see the sea! Montego Bay on Jamaica's north coast was a sleepy little hamlet in the 1950s; today it is a tourist resort of world renown, with an international airport and 7,800 hotel beds.

Schooners in the Careenage, Bridgetown, Barbados

Tricky touchdown—the hill-enclosed runway at Beef Island Airport, British Virgin Islands

Tourism in the West Indies is of two main kinds. On the one hand there are the large modern hotels located usually on the better beaches and catering particularly for richer Americans, and the cruise ships which move from island to island as floating hotels. On the other hand there is a very different kind of tourism, as yet of small importance but growing steadily, which is the movement of West Indians about their own region. They usually stay in the smaller cheaper hotels or in guest houses, and they tend to avoid the main holiday seasons.

It is the first of these kinds of tourism, the big money-spinner, which has caused so much heart-searching: the large modern hotels are designed usually without any regard to their impact on the landscape, or the community in which they are located, but simply to exploit a fine beach or a splendid view. They are foreign-owned as a rule, and not only are the profits sent abroad but the hotels also use mainly imported goods rather than the locally produced ones, so that the benefit to the host country is small. They cater for a class of tourist who all too often seems to have no interest in the culture or in the people of the country he is visiting. But above all this kind of tourism seems to engender undesirable reactions on the part of the people who find employment in the hotels and other facilities. They give up their rural occupations to become waiters or waitresses or taxi-drivers, but at heart they often dislike their servile role. Or they search for ways of separating the tourist from his dollars: the girls may become prostitutes, while the men may become mere hangers-on, hoping to pick up a dollar here or there rather than having to earn a living the hard way. Altogether, if tourism becomes too dominant in a small economy, it can lead to a breakdown in the traditional society and can cause severe disturbance.

The problems of this kind of tourism are now well understood and attempts are being made to counteract them, by insisting on local participation not only financially but in management as well, especially at the higher managerial levels; by insisting on the use of local products such as food, furniture and fittings and building materials; and by trying to encourage the tourist to take an interest in the country and its people. Moreover a determined attempt is now being made to attract tourists from other parts of the world, particularly from Europe, and if they will come at times other than during the main season which runs from mid-December to mid-April, so much the better: it is expected that many of the tourists will prefer the smaller, more 'genuine', type of hotel to the huge 'continental' kind. There is also a movement in the direction of apartment hotels and self-catering bungalows. Rather than that tourism should develop haphazardly, there is a trend now towards more careful forward planning of tourist developments. Dominica, a beautiful island which has hardly experienced much tourism as yet, has had a comprehensive tourism strategy prepared by a firm of consultants who have advised on the areas best suited to hotels and other developments and on the areas where no such development should be permitted. Hopefully, with such a strategy to guide them, Dominica should be able to avoid many of the worst mistakes made by other islands. In Jamaica special efforts are being made to educate the public about the economic importance of tourism, and to help them to understand why they should welcome the visitors, by means of a series of Tourism Matters to You campaigns.

There has been a substantial increase in the number of cruise ships visiting the West Indies in recent years, and in 1970 1.4 million of the 5.6 million tourists visiting the Caribbean were passengers on cruise ships. Especially popular is the 'fly-and-cruise' type of holiday which comprises a flight to the Caribbean plus a cruise and often stay in an hotel. Most of the islands now have deep-water harbours at which these large cruise liners can berth to discharge their passengers. However, this type of tourism is also not without its problems. Often hordes of eager tourists flood into the towns of the smaller islands, gaping at the inhabitants and spending little except to purchase a few inexpensive gifts. The cruise ship is their hotel, where all their meals are served, so that they leave behind little economic benefit to offset the huge capital cost of constructing the deep-water berth.   Jamaica tried to introduce a Cruise Ship Tax in 1969, but the cruise operators reacted by boycotting the Jamaican ports and the Jamaicans had no choice but to woo them back with all kinds of special inducements.

Tourism is now one of the major industries in the West Indies and it is there to stay and to grow. It has given new hope to many islands which had little chance otherwise of ever achieving economic prosperity. It has meant for many people an emancipation from economic slavery in sugar. But its problems cannot be ignored, and the development of the industry in the future must be much more carefully planned and controlled than it has been in the past, if its adverse effects are to be avoided.

5

How They Learn

FORMAL education begins in most Caribbean countries at the age of six and the State does not usually make provision for nursery education. This is therefore left largely to private organisations and as these have to charge fees, the infants of poorer families generally have no formal nursery school education at all. However, in Jamaica, about half the children aged four to six attend some kind of pre-school and of these about 70,000 attend the 'basic schools', ie simple institutions for the children of poorer families which are set up in whatever makeshift accommodation can be found and which receive a small amount of State aid so that the fees charged are within the reach of most families, even the poorest. As in Britain, it is now coming to be realised that the nursery age is of great importance to the later development of the child and in the future, no doubt, this aspect of education will receive more attention than hitherto.

PRIMARY-SECONDARY EDUCATION

There is as much diversity in education facilities among the West Indian islands as there is in most other spheres. At the lower end of the spectrum is as usual Haiti, where about 80 per cent of the people still cannot read or write, and where hitherto there has been little desire on the part of a dictatorial government to educate the people so that they might then be better able to challenge their rulers. Nowhere else in the world is there such a high illiteracy rate. Such education as there is follows the French pattern and is given in French, although the vast majority of the people speak only creole: it also encourages the study of cultural subjects rather than technology or agriculture. 'The whole tradition of élite education is literary, not practical,' wrote Leyburn. 'Teachers trained in this tradition might teach Racine and Montaigne, but not soil conservation and new methods of planting.' Ironically, education in the rural areas is the responsibility of the Ministry of Agriculture (which is notoriously short of funds), while that in the urban areas comes under the Ministry of Education. Although 90 per cent of the children live in rural areas, the number of children from urban areas attending school is greater than that from rural areas—even in the primary schools. Education in Haiti is virtually the monopoly of the rich and the urban classes.

At the other end of the spectrum are countries like Barbados, the Netherlands Antilles, Guadeloupe and Martinique, and Puerto Rico, with excellent schools and with literacy rates over 90 per cent. Barbados has had a high standard of education since the eighteenth century, when Codrington's School and Harrison's Free School were opened. There was a conscious determination to ensure that the children of Barbadian parents would be able to compete on an equal footing with children in the developed countries. As a result the island has the highest literacy rate in the British Commonwealth Caribbean—about 98 per cent. The following statistics show the educational achievements of men and women in the Barbados labour force in 1970:

Education received	Men	Women
Infant or none	324	204
Primary	10,838	7,952
Secondary	31,033	18,230
School Leaving Certificate	2,593	1,646
General Certificate of Education	3,769	3,459

Education received	Men	Women
Diploma	542	365
Degree	750	198
Other	477	575
Not stated	731	295
	51,057	32,924

The Netherlands Antilles have an illiteracy rate of nil and primary education is universal. In Guadeloupe, education is free and compulsory for all children aged from six to sixteen and the children really do attend school (unlike some other islands with notionally compulsory education): the attendance rate is 98 per cent. The education is on French lines and there are three large *lycées* with a total of 5,000 children. It is, however, mainly the children from the urban areas who go to secondary schools: in Martinique for instance two-thirds of the secondary school children are from the main urban centre, Fort de France, which has only one-quarter of the children of school age. As in Haiti, therefore, there is a marked bias in favour of the urban children.

Puerto Rico also has free and compulsory education. The language used in the schools is Spanish, with English as the second language. Children spend six years in the elementary school and another six in the high school. The majority of the children go to the public schools (686,777 children in 1971) but another 87,456 children go to private schools. The latter are gaining in popularity because of the overcrowding in the State schools which is so bad that some of the children can attend only for half days, so that the buildings can be utilised to their maximum capacity.

The remaining West Indian countries generally occupy an intermediate position. Jamaica for instance has free and compulsory education for all children aged from six to fifteen, but the teacher-pupil ratio in the primary schools is 1:54 and many of the teachers are very ill trained. It is perhaps fortunate that only two-thirds of the children on the roll ever turn up for school, since there are simply not enough teachers. Already classes of 50–100 children are not uncommon, often separated from each other only by a thin partition. Teaching by rote is common. The standard of teaching in the high schools is better, but still nothing like as good as in similar schools in Europe or North America, and about 50 per cent of the children fail to get three General Certificate of Education passes. At the time of the 1960 Census of Population, the last for which full census details are available, 15 per cent of the population aged fifteen or more had never attended school, and of the remainder only 7 per cent had received secondary education and only 1 per cent professional. Yet despite these statistics there is among Jamaican children a real keenness to learn and a healthy curiosity about life which probably owes something to the strong Free Church tradition in education in Jamaica. The situation regarding illiteracy is improving rapidly, thanks to a campaign which the government launched recently to eradicate it altogether by 1977, provided always that enough teachers can be trained to overcome the very serious shortage.

The Dominican Republic has adopted the Latin American system of education. Primary education is free and compulsory for all children aged from seven to eleven, but in practice only about one-quarter of all school-age children attend elementary school. There are three stages in education: kindergarten, elementary and higher. The literacy rate is less than 50 per cent and the schools are few in number, understaffed and overcrowded. In 1970 there were only 5,000 primary schools, 75 secondary schools and 500 other schools for a nation of 4·3 million people, of whom 47 per cent are under fifteen years of age. It is small wonder that when the World Bank took a look at the country in 1971, it decided to give priority to a $4 million loan for secondary-school development.

The smaller West Indian islands, such as those in the Windwards and Leewards, have had high illiteracy rates in the past, and outside the towns few of the children ever went to school. Education was in theory free and compulsory, but in practice it was often simply unattainable. There were not enough schools or teachers to go round, and the more remote villages had to do without. About one-quarter of the children in St Lucia never attended school up to quite recent times, and 15 per cent in Dominica. Illiteracy rates were as high as 50 per cent, since although a fairly high proportion of children may have gone to primary school for some years, they left when they had only just started learning and quickly lost even the little they had. However, the situation has improved tremendously in the last two decades. Largely owing to financial aid from Britain, Canada and the USA, many new schools have been built and more teachers trained. In 1972 for instance a new primary school for 800 children was built at Salisbury, Dominica with aid from Britain, while Canada gave the money for St Lucia's first fully comprehensive school. Almost wherever one goes in these islands, one sees new primary and secondary schools, and even though at present they may be grossly understaffed, teachers are gradually being trained and the foundations have been laid for an efficient educational system. The more intelligent children were often sent to Barbados or to Britain for secondary education in the past, but new secondary schools have now been built in the islands and this tradition is dying rapidly.

EDUCATION AND WEST INDIAN CONSCIOUSNESS

The education system of each of the West Indian islands has been closely modelled on that of the 'parent' country, whether British, French, Spanish, Dutch or American. And this applies not only to the system of education but also to the syllabuses used. Nearly all the teaching material originates in Europe or in North America. At one time there was a very good reason for this, since the brighter children who went on to university generally had to go to Europe or to North

America as there were no universities in the West Indies. But this is no longer the case. Moreover, with the achievement of independence in so many islands, there is a new attitude towards education. In the past the teachers were mostly European and they deliberately inculcated in their pupils European values and ideas since these were all they were familiar with —and they genuinely considered them to be superior to other traditions of learning. This was true *par excellence* of the French approach to education. The French had an almost missionary zeal about the desirability of spreading French culture to the developing countries with which they were associated.

With independence has come a more independent attitude of mind on the part of the West Indians. They are no longer content merely to borrow at second hand the ideas and traditions of others: they seek a culture of their own. Nor are they satisfied that their children should use only textbooks published in Europe or North America, based on syllabuses prepared for the children in those countries and dealing with the geography, history, literature and customs of the particular country. Instead they want their children to be taught to appreciate and respect their West Indian culture and traditions: to learn West Indian geography, history, folklore and literature. Once when I was visiting the Carib Reserve in a remote corner of Dominica, I met a Carib schoolboy and asked to see the schoolbooks he was carrying. I read: 'In the winter we make snowmen.' The boy had obviously been using an old English reader. But this boy had never seen snow. Why should he be expected to absorb images totally foreign to his experience?

It is not only a matter of the syllabus but also of the very language itself. In the West Indies the child is not encouraged to use his vernacular because his teacher knows that if he does so in an examination (usually set in London or Cambridge) he will probably be failed. The examiners in England would almost certainly frown on the colourful language that is the everyday means of expression of the Trinidadian or

Jamaican child, with its heavy admixture of American slang derived from a rich diet of American films. So the child is taught to say not 'give a joke' but 'tell a joke': he is made to feel that his way of saying things is somehow wrong. The bias in his teaching is heavily on grammar rather than on comprehension, and the inevitable result is that the child's natural expression is stultified. Steps are now being taken to remedy this situation in the British Commonwealth countries and the Ministers of Education of these countries, together with representatives of the University of the West Indies, have been discussing the setting up of a Caribbean Examinations Council to prepare for the assumption of responsibility for the setting, conduct and administration of examinations at the secondary level.

The fact is that independence has wrought a deep and fundamental change in attitudes towards education. The ex-colonial powers regarded education more or less as a social service, ie as the expression of a sense of social responsibility towards subject peoples. But today education is seen more as the cement of national pride and dignity and as building the economic fibre of the nation. Modern education is regarded as a vital investment in the future by countries which lack above all the skills to develop their own resources as independent states. Seen in this light, much of the existing education in the West Indies seems to be misdirected. It inculcates expatriate concepts and values and it is geared to academic achievement rather than to developing skills of potential use to society. Primary schools are still regarded mainly as a preparation for secondary school, but the great majority of children never go to secondary school in many West Indian countries, or if they do, they do not complete their education and drop out with virtually no vocational skills of value to the community. People are beginning to question the whole structure of the educational system and to ask whether it really is the kind that meets the requirements of the West Indies in present circumstances.

THE UNIVERSITIES

With the exception of the French and Netherlands Antilles, where young people going on to university generally have to complete their studies in Europe, all the larger West Indian islands now have their own universities and the smaller ones can use the facilities of the bigger ones.

University-level education in the West Indies dates back to 1538, with the foundation in what is now the Dominican Republic, of the Universidad de Santo Domingo, the oldest institution for higher education in the Americas. This university now has over 5,000 students. There are also two smaller universities, the Universidad Pedro Hernandez Urena, also in Santo Domingo and the Catholic and apolitical (students at the other two universities are highly politically motivated) Universidad Madre y Maestra in Santiago de los Caballeros. This was founded in 1962 and, following its move to a new site in 1967, is now capable of accommodating about 1,000 students.

If the Dominican Republic has the oldest university in the West Indies, Puerto Rico has by far the largest. Founded in 1903, the University of Puerto Rico now has over 30,000 students (with plans for further expansion) which makes it one of the largest centres for advanced study in the Americas. It has a beautifully situated main campus at Rio Piedras, south of San Juan and subsidiary campuses at Mayaguez (which possesses a nuclear reactor) and at Ponce. In addition, the Catholic University at Ponce has 6,500 students and the Inter-American University, with its main campuses at San Juan and San German and five colleges elsewhere, has 10,000 students. The World University in San Juan has 1,300 students. In common with all other institutions for advanced learning in the West Indies, the University of Puerto Rico tries to instil an interest and pride in all things West Indian: to further this aim the university established in 1955 an Institute of Culture, with the specific objective of encouraging an interest in Puerto Rican culture. The university also houses the well-known Institute of Caribbean Studies which has sponsored an excellent series of scholarly studies of social, political and economic aspects of West Indian life.

In the British Commonwealth islands, students now read for degrees at the University of the West Indies, established in 1962. Although the university has not grown rapidly in size (it has about 5,000 students) a high standard of teaching has been maintained. The founders of the university believed that quality was more important than quantity, and this philosophy has guided the university leaders ever since. There are three main campuses: at Mona, beautifully situated in a basin in the hills at the back of Kingston; at St Augustine, Port of Spain, where the old Imperial College of Tropical Agriculture (founded in 1924) was situated; and at Cave Hill, Barbados, where the College of Arts and Sciences was established in 1968 (after having been located temporarily in Bridgetown since 1963). The University of the West Indies also has a Department of Extramural Studies at Nassau in the Bahamas, and another at Roseau, Dominica. Like the University of Puerto Rico, the University of the West Indies has established a number of special offshoots to foster Caribbean studies, and these include the new Institute of International Relations in Trinidad. In Barbados there is a Centre for Multiracial Studies which has links with the University of Sussex in Britain, and which has recently completed a comparative study of ethnic differences between Barbados and St Vincent. The Centre houses the Richard Moore collection of 15,000 volumes covering the history and culture of peoples of African descent.

The University of the West Indies is unique in that it serves a wide variety of islands of different size and spanning a huge area. The original capital was provided partly by grants from individual West Indian governments and partly from private sources: recurrent expenditure is met from contributions from the British Commonwealth governments on a proportionate basis related to population. Although the Federation itself collapsed in 1962, the university survived and the governments continued their contributions, except that Guyana dropped out in 1963 as it had decided to set up a university of its own, and the Bahamas stepped in to take its place. The need to satisfy fourteen different governments leads at times to considerable tension, as what may pass for academic freedom in one island may be called political subversion in another. In the early days most of the professors and lecturers were European or American, but during the 1960s West Indianisation proceeded rapidly and the expatriates have now either left or are kept very much in the background. With the students in their present mood of West Indian assertiveness, anything that savours of academic imperialism is unacceptable. Many hopes were dashed by the failure of the Federation but the success of the university is a reminder of the great ideals which lay behind the Federation idea, and may indicate that they are not dead but dormant. A meeting of heads of governments of Commonwealth Caribbean countries in 1972 confirmed that the University of the West Indies would continue to be the regional institution for higher learning. An important development in the direction of regional co-operation was the establishment in 1968 of the Association of Caribbean Universities (which includes the USA since it borders the Caribbean area).

In Haiti, university education began with the establishment in Port au Prince of the State University in 1944. It has ten faculties and is run on American lines, although many of the professors are from the Institut Français in France. Despite the overwhelming agricultural nature of Haiti's economy, the students mostly study law or medicine. There is a surplus of doctors and lawyers in the towns although not in the rural areas. There are about 2,000 students.

Among the smaller islands there are a few small colleges which offer university-level training of a specialised kind. In the American Virgin Islands for instance the College of the Virgin Islands in St Thomas offers degree courses: it has a few hundred full-time students and a rather larger number of part-time students. In the Netherlands Antilles the practice is still for most students to go to the Netherlands for their university education, but a law school has now been opened in Curaçao. Similarly in the French Antilles students generally go to France, although they can now study law and economics to university level at the Institut Vizioz and sciences at the Centre d'Etudes Supérieures Scientifiques, while a new Centre Universitaire Antill-Guyanes is currently being established. As time goes by, therefore, the dependence of these islands on metropolitan facilities will be diminished.

TECHNICAL EDUCATION

In parallel with the new pattern of thinking about the role of education in recent years, there has been a growing concern with the inadequacy of existing technical and vocational training facilities in the West Indies. In virtually all the smaller islands until recently there were no facilities at all for vocational training, with the result that there was a desperate shortage of skilled workers of all kinds.

It was to remedy this situation that drastic steps were taken a few years ago in most of the smaller islands to establish technical institutes and vocational training schools. For example Britain agreed to help finance the building of seven technical colleges in the Leeward and Windward Islands and these have all now been completed. Today there are new technical colleges in St Lucia, St Vincent, St Kitts, Montserrat, Grenada, Dominica and Antigua. Typical of the others is the St Kitts College, with 120 full-time students and about 50 day-release students, learning a wide range of skills including mechanical, motor and agricultural engineering, joinery, masonry, electrical installation, air-conditioning and refrigeration, hotel trades and commercial studies. In three years from 1969 to 1972 the number of students receiving technical education in these associated states has risen from nil to about 1,000. These new colleges are instilling a sense of pride and achievement in craftsmanship. 'It will be the aim of the

college', says the announcement of the opening of the St
Vincent College, 'to dispel the erroneous and out-of-date
notion that the acquiring of technical skills should be reserved
for only the less intellectually gifted.'

As to the larger islands, they have had a small technical
education system for much longer, but it was totally inadequate to meet the needs and they all have large expansion
programmes. In 1971 for instance the Government of Trinidad announced plans for the building of fifteen vocational
training schools (to supplement the John Donaldson Technical Institute in Port of Spain and the San Fernando
Technical Institute) at a total cost of T/T $24 million. Trini-
dad has also developed a number of specialised adult and
vocational education centres, such as the Cipriani Labour
College, which aims to develop a responsible and mature
labour movement and which moved into new buildings at
Valsayn in 1972, and the Productivity Centre which provides
training at all levels of modern management. These supplement the normal adult training classes held at the
community centres in Trinidad and which the government
has gone out of its way to encourage in recent years. With
unemployment problems very much in mind the government
has also launched a programme to stimulate interest in local
handicrafts and cottage industries.

With all this effort in the field of technical education, one
might assume that the problem is well on the way to being
solved. But in practice things have not worked out quite as
planned. On the one hand people are finding that as soon as
they have acquired a skill they can earn twice or three times
as much in the USA as in the West Indies and they promptly
emigrate. In Trinidad and Tobago for example 696 nurses
were trained during the period 1965–9, but during this same
period 586 resigned and emigrated . . . and this was after the
British Government had drastically limited immigration into
Britain. On the other hand there are signs that more people
are being trained in certain trades and skills than can possibly
find employment in their own islands. Everyone wants to be a

motor mechanic and no one wants to learn agricultural skills. There will soon be more motor mechanics than motor vehicles in the islands! However, to some extent this problem may be merely part of the growing pains to be expected of any new change in policy.

During the great expansion of primary and secondary education that took place during the 1950s and 1960s, when there was such an acute shortage of teachers, standards of teacher-training were often abysmally low. Without a substantial number of expatriate teachers the expansion programme would not have been possible. However, it was clearly undesirable to continue for too long with white faces in front of the blackboards and urgent steps were taken to increase the number of locally trained teachers. In Jamaica for instance in 1961 the number of those trained locally was 230: in 1970 it was about 1,000, and by 1975 it will be 1,400. Bearing in mind however that the number of children in secondary schools trebled between 1962 and 1970, even this rate of increase did not produce much improvement in the pupil-teacher ratio. Jamaica's six teacher-training colleges have 136 teachers and 1,876 trainees (1,528 of them women), a ratio of 1 : 13·7. There is also a training college for junior teachers at Caenwood, with 7 teachers and 107 students. Trinidad also had a crash programme for teacher-training ever since it obtained independence in 1962.

The smaller islands have solved their problems of scale either by sending the trainees to Europe (eg from the Netherlands Antilles, although there is now a small teacher-training college in Curaçao, or by organising centralised facilities in one island to serve the neighbouring ones. Thus the Leeward Islands Training College at Golden Grove, Antigua (recently modernised) trains student teachers from Dominica, the British Virgin Islands, Montserrat and Antigua with a two-year post-GCE course. Dominica, however, has decided to set

H

up its own teacher-training college, while the other Windward and Leeward Islands, the Bahamas and Barbados already have their own. The Institute of Education, University of the West Indies established in 1963, has an important role in improving teacher-training facilities.

YOUTH CAMPS

Throughout the Commonwealth Caribbean, but particularly in Jamaica where the International Labour Organisation of the United Nations is engaged on a two-year programme to sponsor them, there are special youth camps where young people aged from fifteen to twenty spend twelve to eighteen months learning a skill. The primary aim is to teach youngsters a trade so that they will be able to find employment when they leave the camp, and of the 20,000 young people who have passed through the camps in Jamaica since they started in 1955 about 75 per cent have found employment. In 1971 Jamaica had five youth camps, one of them for girls, with 1,600 campers. There are youth camps also in Trinidad and Dominica.

The youth camps are undoubtedly filling an important need in the Caribbean, but it must be remembered that they are really necessary only because the educational system has failed to equip school-leavers with even the basic skills to do a useful job in the community. First priority should therefore be given to improving the educational system. Then the youth camps could be used for what should be their main purpose of recreation and character training, rather than as vocational training schools in disguise.

LIBRARIES

Barbados makes the proud claim that it established a free public library three years before Britain and one year before the USA (1847). But this early promise was not sustained.

There was little or no progress, and library services in Barbados and indeed throughout the Caribbean, remained very rudimentary until recently. It was only with the attack on illiteracy and the great improvement in education made during the post-war period that library services began to be more efficient. New and attractive buildings were erected and the stock of books was much improved. In each of the thirteen parishes in Jamaica a new and attractive library has been built in the last decade, and all three branches of Trinidad's Central Library have been provided with new buildings. The three university campuses have each been given excellent library facilities. Only Montserrat, St Kitts and Antigua still have inadequate library premises. Another important development was that the books were taken to the people rather than wait for the people to come to the books. Small collections of popular books have been established at places frequented by the public, such as shops, schools, government offices—even private houses; and mobile libraries, or 'bookmobiles', have been introduced with great success. These are now in use in Grenada, Barbados, St Lucia, Trinidad and Tobago and Jamaica, and they are particularly popular with the young people. The bookmobile in Barbados, which was started in 1963, has 2,400 books and it visits twenty-five sites fortnightly. There is also a schools mobile service which was established in 1969: visits to fifty-nine schools are made every three weeks and the library contains 3,000 books.

Much improved though they are, the library facilities are still inadequate by European standards, particularly in terms of the number of books available which is less than one per head of the population on average. The libraries of Jamaica have only about 1 million books to 2 million people. No more than 15 per cent of the population are registered readers, and in Jamaica each registered reader borrows about six books a year on average. Although the situation regarding trained library staff is very much better than it was in the early 1930s, when there were no trained librarians at all in the British West Indies, there are still only just over 100 to serve about

4 million people. On the basis of the standard in developed countries there ought to be 265 at an absolute minimum. However, the situation should be much improved in the future as a new library school has now been set up in the University of the West Indies at Kingston which will train thirty undergraduates on a three-year course, plus a number of post-graduate one-year diploma students. Perhaps what is needed now most of all are more books dealing with the Caribbean for the libraries to lend.

6

How They Get About

SEA TRANSPORT

LIKE islanders everywhere, the West Indians have traditionally been good seamen and the sea has always been in their
blood. Until recently the majority of the Cayman Islanders for
instance were merchant seamen serving all over the world.
There are many coastal villages still on the more mountainous
islands which have poor road communications and depend
almost entirely on sea travel. Haiti is a case in point: it has
850 miles of coastline and although the small boats used may
have a high propensity for sinking, they are still more effective
than land transport over rutted dirt roads. The original Carib
people of the Leewards and Windwards were renowned for
their seamanship and 'canoe' is itself a West Indian word. The
Spaniards learned to fear the huge Carib war canoes that
could outpace their own galleons. To this day the islanders on
the windswept Atlantic coasts handle their canoes with con-
summate skill and courage, and although the boats are quite
frequently overturned in the surf, it is rare that lives are lost.

Canoes are still widely used, but they have been mostly
superseded for commercial purposes by rather larger boats
fitted with outboard motors, or by the traditional schooners
that still ply in considerable numbers between the islands
carrying light cargoes of all kinds. It is seldom that a West
Indian harbour is without a schooner or two loading or
unloading, and they are always a picturesque element of the
Caribbean scene. The schooners are still built in the Grenadines, particularly Bequia and Carriaçou, as they have been

for generations. Some of them are now motorised, such as the regular mail-boats serving St Vincent and the Grenadines, and also the various ferries.

Inter-island ferries play an important part in the life of the West Indies and they often carry substantial numbers of people. When one such ferry, the *Christena*, plying between St Kitts and Nevis, went down on 1 August 1970, only 92 of the 292 passengers survived. She had operated a daily service since 1958. Although navigation between the islands is normally reasonably safe and pleasant, there are hazards in the form of hurricanes and uncharted reefs. The foundering of the crack French liner *Antilles* (20,000 tons) on a reef near the island of Mustique in the Grenadines is a reminder of the dangers. This disaster was attributed to the general inadequacy of marine channels and the lack of warning beacons for dangerous reefs. In August 1973 the liner *Canberra* was blown aground by high winds in the harbour of St Thomas in the American Virgin Islands, but she successfully refloated herself.

One of the busiest ferries in the Caribbean is that between Miami and Freeport in the Bahamas operated by two ships, the 14,000ton MV *Freeport* and her sister ship the MV *Grand Bahama*. A new ferry service, started in the summer of 1973, operates between Aruba, Curaçao, Bonaire and Venezuela and carries 300 cars and 800 passengers. This is only a short sea route and may well operate at a profit. On the longer ferry routes, however, there has been difficulty in making profits, and Fyffes for example have withdrawn their passenger service between Jamaica and Bermuda, using the SS *Camito*, because of the rise in operating costs and the fall in profit margins. The ability to carry cars probably makes a big difference to profit margins. New forms of ferry service are now being tried out, the most interesting being the fast hydrofoil service between the British Virgin Islands and the American Virgin Islands using the 116-passenger Russian-built Comet hydroliner. There are now plans to provide a similar service in the Grenadines using a Rocket hydroliner.

As standards of living rise in the West Indies, so there is much more travel by the local people themselves. The greatest spur to interisland travel was the decision of the Canadian Government at the time of the West Indian Federation (1961) to donate two ships for the specific purpose of operating a regular schedule of sailings from island to island. These were the *Federal Maple* and *Federal Palm*. They were each 2,800 gross registered tons and were operated by the West Indies Shipping Corporation (WISC). They carried both cargo and passengers and ran a fortnightly service between Trinidad and Jamaica, sailing from island to island. Unfortunately these two ships were never a paying proposition and in 1972 it was decided to sell the *Federal Palm* to the Republic of Nauru in the Pacific; but the *Federal Maple* was given refurbished passenger accommodation and will continue in service. At the same time the WISC has introduced a new 1,500ton container ship and another is due to come into service shortly. If these can reduce the time spent in port, they may prove commercially successful.

The larger vessels seen in West Indian ports are either cruise ships or cargo vessels: usually banana or sugar boats, bulk carriers for bauxite, or oil tankers; and sometimes one sees general tramp ships carrying a wide range of small cargoes. As described in Chapter 4, the number of cruise ships using West Indian harbours is increasing all the time. In 1972 regular cruises were being run to the Caribbean by fifteen lines from the USA (excluding five to the Bahamas only), seven from Britain and another five from Caribbean ports. Taking Jamaica as an example, during 1971 a total of 137 cruise ships called at Jamaican ports. The market is growing at about 10 per cent per annum and more facilities for cruise ships are being installed at several West Indian ports. The cruise ships apart, there are no regular passenger services left now between Europe or North America and the West Indies, except the restricted passenger facilities offered in the banana boats, and the few other cargo boats which also have limited passenger accommodation. The eight refrigerated Geest banana boats have very good accommodation for twelve passengers, and Fyffes can also accommodate passengers in their four twelve-berth banana boats. Other lines which sail between Europe or North America and the West Indies are the Saguenay Shipping Company, Fratelli Grimaldi Line, Harrison Line, Atlantic Line, Booker Seaway and the Blue Ribbon Line. An interesting recent development is that the Grenada Government is reported to be looking into the possibility of establishing 'flag-of-convenience' facilities for registering ships along the lines of those operating in Panama and Liberia. Oil tankers get bigger every year and in 1973 Shell Oil in Curaçao announced plans for the construction of a massive new oil terminal with a pier capable of handling tankers of 500,000 tons.

HARBOURS AND PORTS

The continued improvement in sea-transport facilities in the West Indies depends very much on the improvement of ports and harbours. Some of these are still very primitive and incapable of taking large vessels or handling substantial traffic. Dominica for instance still has no deep-water harbour and the small jetty at Roseau is useless except for schooners and small coasters. All goods have to be loaded or unloaded by lighter which is costly, slow and sometimes hazardous. Haiti has a dozen ports along its extensive coastline but only one or two of them are adequately equipped to handle sea traffic.

However, during the last decade, there have been some important developments and new deep-water harbours have been built in several places. Such a harbour was built in 1960–1 at Bridgetown, Barbados, capable of taking eight ocean-going ships, together with huge storage sheds for raw sugar and bulk-handling equipment for loading the sugar. Before that the smaller vessels used the picturesque but rather impractical careenage, and the larger ones anchored out in Carlisle Bay while lighters plied to and fro. The new harbour has attracted an important *entrepôt* trade to Barbados, so that already it handles more than twice the 160,000 tons per annum for which it was designed and plans are now afoot for an extension. New deep-water harbours have also been built at St Johns, Antigua (1968) where an 18,000ft channel was dredged to a depth of 35ft to enable the cruise liners to come alongside; at Port Purcell near Roadtown in the British Virgin Islands (completed in 1972); and at Freeport in Grand Bahama, built in 1959 and now one of the largest artificial harbours in the world. Plans are going ahead for new deep-water harbours in Dominica (at Woodbridge Bay near Roseau) and in the Cayman Islands, where passenger liners seldom call at present because berthing facilities are not available. Even the tiny island of St Eustatius (921 people) is being given a new landing stage 100m long and 12m wide.

Major harbour improvements are planned for a number of Caribbean ports. Castries, St Lucia, one of the safest anchorages in the West Indies, is to have a new deep-water berth which will be able to accommodate the increasing number of cruise liners now visiting the port. Big improvements are taking place also at Kingstown, St Vincent, where harbour extension and deepening work are being carried out to provide berths for cruise liners. In Port of Spain, Trinidad, which is an excellent natural harbour and safe anchorage, a 7,000ft access channel is being dredged off Sealots, together with a 3,000ft by 800ft turning basin; and a major fishing complex is being built, covering an area of 40 acres and providing berthing facilities for 500 deep-sea trawlers and 600 smaller craft. Part of this important redevelopment scheme too is a proposal to establish a large container port, which will handle the container traffic of the South Caribbean and also act as a feeder port for Latin American countries. Containerisation is already a feature of sea traffic out of San Juan and Port au Prince, but as yet it has not made much headway elsewhere in the Caribbean, although the Geest banana boats have been adapted to handle 'unitised' cargoes from Britain to the West Indies (ie miscellaneous cargo arranged in convenient 'units' for ready loading and unloading rather than being stowed loose).

At Kingston, Jamaica, a magnificent natural harbour and the seventh largest in the world, far-reaching harbour improvements are now being made. Roll-on roll-off facilities are being provided to accommodate two vessels simultaneously, with 3,000ft of lateral berthing, 35ft of depth alongside and 30 acres of storage space. More important still is the J $30 million project announced recently by the Jamaican Government to establish Kingston as the major transhipment port of the Caribbean. The new installations will be alongside the modern deep-water docks at Newport West. Kingston's port facilities will soon be the most modern and efficient in the Caribbean.

There are other ports and harbours in addition to those already mentioned, chiefly of course San Juan, a major port which has increased vastly in importance and commerce since Puerto Rico's economic expansion. Nassau in the Bahamas has a magnificent natural harbour capable of taking ships up to 35,000 tons moored alongside. Port Antonio, Jamaica's chief banana port (soon to have a new deep-water pier) and Santo Domingo, the Dominican Republic's busy port but the only one of any consequence in the country apart from Pedernales, the bauxite terminal, are other important West Indian ports.

AIR TRANSPORT

It was Pan Am which pioneered air travel in the West Indies when it introduced a regular flight from Miami to San Juan in the 1930s: before that the most satisfactory route had been by boat from New York. World War II intervened and in some ways delayed the natural development of air travel in the region, but in other ways gave it an important boost. Two large new military airfields were built by the USA at strategic locations in the West Indies, one at Beanfield near Vieux Fort in St Lucia, and the other at Coolidge, Antigua. The first of these was handed to the St Lucian Government in 1960 and after modernisation, extension and re-equipping, was opened for normal traffic in 1970, making St Lucia the only island in the Eastern Caribbean with two commercial airports. The smaller of the two, at Vigie near Castries, can take only the smaller planes, but Beanfield, now known by its ancient Carib name of Hewanorra, can accommodate the large Boeings and Tristar on its 9,000ft runway, a gift from the Canadian Government. BOAC now flies direct twice-weekly services from London to St Lucia, and Court Line is developing a major tourist business on the island using its own planes and flying the tourists direct from Britain. So the war certainly advanced the cause of air travel faster in St Lucia than would have been likely in the natural course of events.

As to the other military airfield, Coolidge in Antigua, this was handed over to the island authorities after the war and quickly became an important focal point for air routes in the Eastern Caribbean since it was the largest airfield in the region at one time. In 1970 the runway was enlarged to 9,000ft and it can now take the large modern jets flying direct from Europe. It was the existence of this airfield that gave Antigua a head start in the development of its tourist industry and the island is now one of the principal tourist centres of the Windward and Leeward Islands. It is doubtful whether Antigua would have achieved this importance as a tourist centre had it not been for the building of the wartime military airfield there.

During the post-war period, the network of airways was extended gradually so that today every small island is linked into the system by some means or other, and even the smallest islands have airlines of their own—in fact the possession of a 'national' airline has become almost a matter of vital prestige. Virtually all of them are running at a substantial loss, and some of them will probably last for only a short period. Air Dominica for example lasted for only a year or two before going into liquidation, and Air Montserrat, with its single DC3, is another small airline that has gone bankrupt recently. Even the larger airlines find difficulty in remaining solvent.

Bahamas Airways, with 900 employees and 800 flights per week, went into voluntary liquidation in 1970. Another large airline in the region which has been in considerable difficulties is Caribair, the major Puerto Rican airline, and it has been taken over recently by Eastern Airways.

One of the leading airlines is LIAT, or Leeward Islands Air Transport, which began in 1956 with one Piper Apache aircraft and now operates regular daily services throughout the Eastern Caribbean from Trinidad up to Puerto Rico, serving twenty-four islands in all. Until recently, the aircraft most in use was an Avro 748. It is seldom in the air long enough between islands to reach its normal cruising height, let alone to allow the attractive air hostesses in their sheeny silk outfits to serve a meal. It is up and down, up and down, all the way along the chain of islands, and the route is known throughout the region as the 'island-hopping' one. On average the planes make fifteen take-offs and landings each day, and this makes LIAT the 'busiest' airline in the world. It also adds greatly to the airline's operating costs, as there are fees to be paid each time. It is small wonder then that LIAT made losses for many years and these were reputed to be of the order of £1 million per annum. In 1972 LIAT was taken over by Court's, the large British shipping and travel group, and the main change that has occurred as a result is that the Avro aircraft have been supplemented by the larger BAC 111s which can carry more passengers although they cannot as yet land on all the smaller islands. It will be very interesting to see whether Court's, with its great experience in the air-travel business, will be able to make the airline a commercial success, or whether the immutable facts of geography will defeat the company.

Finding suitable sites for airfields is one of the basic problems in the smaller and more mountainous islands of the West Indies. Often the terrain is so hilly that it is virtually impossible to find enough flat land for an airfield of the required length. The classic case is Dominica. Landing at Melville Hall is a most unnerving experience. The Avro 748, the largest aircraft which can land there, circles the edge of the bowl in the mountains, almost scraping the tall coconut trees, and touches down on a runway which merges into the surf of the Atlantic ocean. Fortunately, night flying is not allowed there! Yet this site, inconvenient as it is (it is about 40 miles from the capital), seems to be the only one possible on the island, which is one of the largest in the Eastern Caribbean. There have been suggestions that an alternative site might be Brantridge, on the so-called Layou Flats near the centre of the island, and a meteorological station has been set up there to take readings, but as it lies at a height of about 2,000ft in an area which has almost constant cloud-cover and rainfall over 200in a year, the chances of its proving suitable seem very slim. Dominica is likely to be stuck with Melville Hall for many years yet.

There are several other islands that have small and inconvenient airfields which cannot readily be enlarged to accommodate larger aircraft. These are St Vincent (Arnos Vale Airport, but the Government in 1973 purchased Langley Park estate, 24 miles from Kingstown, with a view to building a new international airport there); the British Virgin Islands (Beef Island Airport which was recently given a much needed new terminal building); Tobago (Scarborough Airport); Anguilla (Wall Blake Airport); Montserrat; the Turks and Caicos; and the outlying islands of the Bahamas with their fifty-five airfields and landing strips. It is very unlikely that any of these can be enlarged to take the big aircraft and if the present tendency for the Avro 748 to be superseded by the larger jets continues, these small islands may find themselves isolated. An example of this occurred recently in the Western Caribbean, where British West Indian Airlines (BWIA) decided to pull out of the Cayman Islands because the company had switched from the smaller Boeing 727s to the 707s and these could not land at Owen Roberts Airport, Grand Cayman. The writing may be on the wall for the smaller West Indian islands. 'Small' may be 'beautiful'—but it can also be lonely.

The larger islands too are not without their problems. The Dominican Republic for instance has a quite extensive internal airline network serving the larger cities and towns, but as yet the number of domestic passengers is too small to enable the airline to run at a profit and its future is very uncertain. In Haiti there are internal airline connections between Port au Prince and seven other cities, with several flights a week, but these are being operated at present by the military and a recent consultants' report on the development of the island's tourist industry strongly urges that the airline be run on a normal commercial basis, since visitors do not find it altogether reassuring, in a country with Haiti's reputation, to be ferried about by the military! In Puerto Rico there are internal flights connecting the main cities, while large helicopters and light aircraft are used to transport tourists from the airport at San Juan (a magnificent building, of a size which dwarfs any other in the West Indies) to their hotels in the interior. In Jamaica also small aircraft are used (mainly Twin Otters) to link the main cities and to transport tourists, but the services are rudimentary at present. The fact is that most of the Caribbean islands are too small to justify regular internal air routes and the greatest emphasis, rightly, has gone into improving the roads.

So far as international air connections are concerned, the West Indies are probably better served than any other comparable area in the world. Because of the many nations with interests in the region, there are many international carriers which operate regular services to the West Indies, and of course the growing tourist trade gives the islands an importance far greater than their mere size would appear to warrant. There are large modern international airports capable of taking Boeing 707s (although not all of them are capable yet of taking the Boeing Jumbo 747) in all the more important islands.

Looking into the future, there is likely to be a continued improvement in the airports of the West Indies, with each island vying with the others to offer the best and most up-to-date facilities to encourage the international airlines to use their airports. Major improvements are planned for Jamaica's two existing airports, while a third international airport at Ocho Rios on the north coast is also being considered. The smaller islands will intensify their efforts to improve their facilities mainly for the sake of their tourist industries, although it may be that if aircraft requiring shorter runways for landing and take-off are introduced, their relative position will be improved. The smallest among them will have to recognise that they cannot join the big league and must search for ways of counteracting the adverse effects of isolation. Thus Nevis has shown the way with its acquisition, in 1973, of a ten-seater helicopter and the establishment of the first heliport in the Caribbean. Whether the trend for larger aircraft on internal routes can go much further seems doubtful, as the distances between the islands are too short to allow the large aircraft to be used efficiently—already they seem to be operating at well below capacity, with many unoccupied seats. The one certain fact is that air travel will always be a more integral part of the lives of the West Indians than of most other people in the world, and many of them will learn to 'fly' even before they learn to walk.

ROADS AND ROAD TRANSPORT

There is a wide range in the inadequacy of the road networks in the West Indian islands. Haiti has very poor roads indeed outside the main towns, and even the inter-city roads are often in a deplorable condition. Until it was rebuilt recently, the main road in the country, linking Port au Prince with the second city, Cap Haitien, was appallingly bad. The best road is the one which every visitor sees—that from the airport to the city of Port au Prince, but elsewhere the roads are pitted with potholes and if they are surfaced at all it tends to be with rough *pavé* which merely ensures that an average speed of 16mph is good going. Outside the towns, vehicles are rare and donkeys are the main form of transport. Donkeys were indeed once the principal means of transport in other West Indian islands but they have now mostly disappeared: animal transport is rarely seen, apart of course from those tourist attractions, the surreys of Nassau. In the towns of Haiti the most numerous vehicles, apart from lorries and vans, are the various kinds of bus and taxi, including the 'publique' taxis which ply between the towns on regular schedules; the 'camionettes' which are usually trucks fitted with seats and painted in bright colours, with flamboyant symbols, slogans and names; and the 'L' taxis (so-called from the letter L in the number plate) which are the official tourist cabs operating at set government rates (about twenty times more expensive than other forms of transport!). But mostly it is people and animals one sees using the roads. Everywhere, as in India, there are people walking about, often carrying heavy loads over long distances—particularly vegetables and other produce for sale in the towns. Life in Haiti is always hard, and a great deal of it is spent on the roads—but not in cars.

Roads also are generally inadequate in the other mountainous islands, because the costs of roadbuilding have been such that there were seldom sufficient funds in the budget. During the past twenty years, however, overseas aid has been widely used for road construction and this has made an enormous difference. In Dominica for instance British aid enabled the transinsular road (known rather grandiloquently as the Imperial Road) to be completed in the 1950s, linking the new airport at Melville Hall with the capital, and it is currently being used to construct the major new road along the coast from Roseau to Portsmouth as well as a number of other roads in the island. In St Lucia British aid is being used to improve the road link from Castries to Vieux Fort, and in St Vincent (which still has no transinsular road) the Leeward Highway is being refurbished at a total cost of EC $2 million.

The torrential rains that are experienced in some of the more mountainous islands cause many serious landslips, and bridges and roads are frequently washed away or damaged. The rivers can rise as much as 25ft overnight and roadworks have to be constructed to cope with these extreme conditions. The British Virgin Islands are particularly subject to these damaging storms and in 1970 the main road from Roadtown to West End was damaged so badly that the cost of repair was US $120,000 (£48,000). This is a heavy burden for an island of only a few thousand people. It not infrequently happens that roads built by European contractors who are not familiar with tropical storms suffer particularly badly because inadequate culverts are provided to cope with the rapid run-off.

The road system in the larger islands is much more developed than in the smaller ones, especially in Puerto Rico and Trinidad which have excellent road systems. Puerto Rico for instance has over 4,000 miles of tarred roads, and there are over 600,000 vehicles on the island, or about one vehicle to every four inhabitants, ie say one per family. This puts Puerto Rico about on a par with Britain, for instance. Trinidad, which is said to have the best road system in the West Indies, has over 2,000 miles of roads, and over 90,000 vehicles or one vehicle for every eleven inhabitants. Jamaica has a good system, as indeed have most of the islands that were part of the British West Indies, but the maintenance is not very good. The Netherlands Antilles also have excellent roads, as one might expect from the extraordinarily high rate of car ownership—about one car for every three inhabitants. Martinique has 440 miles of good tarred roads, including some modern expressways and there are over 50,000 vehicles (one vehicle to every seven inhabitants). The roads in the French Antilles are classified in the same way as those in France, ie as *routes nationales* or *routes départementales* apart from the few autoroutes and expressways. The Dominican Republic has a network of four-lane highways radiating out from Santo Domingo and anyone in the republic with a car should be able to drive to the capital within twenty-four hours. Because of the friction with Haiti, however, road connections with

I

that country are still very poor. In Barbados there are 726 miles of tarred roads which give that island one of the highest road densities anywhere in the world; the only snag is that the roads were laid out in the horse-and-buggy era and their alignments are often very bad. There are few pavements and the pedestrian walks in constant danger of his life. Recently there has been a sharp increase in the number of motor cycles in use and, sadly, in the number of young people involved in accidents as a result of the narrow and overcrowded roads.

Buses still play a very important part in the lives of most West Indians, especially those in the lower-income groups, and in many cases they are desperately overcrowded. In Jamaica in 1969 there were 413 buses and they carried 148 million passengers over 319 miles of routes; but the vehicles are sometimes antiquated and the services leave much to be desired. In Barbados only about 15 per cent of the people own a car and another 2½ per cent a motor cycle, so most people depend heavily on the bus services; as over half the families in the island live within 200 yards of public transport, this presents no problems . . . except at rush-hours when fighting one's way on to a bus (queueing is one thing the Bajans never learned from the British) is quite an experience. Not many white people or tourists care to travel by bus for this reason. Bus services in the French islands are called *transport en commun* or, in creole, simply *le voi,* and the buses will stop anywhere at the wave of a hand; fares are ridiculously low. In Puerto Rico most people use the *publicos* for journeys into the country areas. These are five-seater taxis which operate on scheduled routes and will stop anywhere en route—and even sometimes off it! In the smaller and poorer islands the buses are often simply lorries fitted with seats, but modern buses are gradually being introduced, as in Dominica during the last year or two. Few of the islands have cities large enough for extensive urban bus services to be necessary, but in San Juan there are excellent modern buses which help to give the city its metropolitan air: some of them are even air-conditioned, although double the fare is charged in consequence. In Santo Domingo, for some curious reason, the buses are double-deckers, but the service is hopelessly antiquated and inadequate for this fast-growing city and its ever expanding suburbs. The only other West Indian island with double-deckers is Grand Bahama where a few ply in Freeport mainly for the benefit of the tourists. In St Lucia, as in other islands, the buses bear colourful slogans such as 'Why worry?' or 'God's delight'.

Bicycles are a common form of transport on the flatter islands, particularly Barbados, the Bahamas and Antigua. Taxis are also a common form of transport throughout the West Indies, much more so than in Europe or North America. In Trinidad for example there are no less than 5,000 registered taxis, and even so the government issued an order in 1973 sanctioning another 1,000 taxis. On Grand Bahama the taxi-drivers' union is so strong that it has a virtual monopoly of passenger transport; there are a few buses, but they do not operate a fixed schedule.

In the islands of the British West Indies traffic moves on the left-hand side of the road, as in Britain, even in the Bahamas where most of the vehicles have left-hand drive! Elsewhere, however, traffic moves on the right.

Looking to the future, the main problem on the roads, as in so many other parts of the world, is likely to be that of traffic congestion. Already there are traffic jams, meters, multi-storey car-parks, traffic police, car lots, used-car dumps and all the paraphernalia of the motor-car age; while the rate of increase in car ownership is such that congestion is certain to grow at an alarming rate and faster than the roads and other facilities can be improved. If the West Indies is not to suffer the environmental pollution that has been the fate of the more affluent countries, action must be taken now to prevent the situation from worsening. A really good public transport system is probably the most urgent need, and until it can be achieved, traffic congestion and pollution are likely to get worse.

THE RAILWAYS

Railways have played a relatively minor role in the development of communications in the West Indies, for obvious reasons. The islands are simply too small as a rule to justify rail transport. Only in the larger islands such as Puerto Rico, Hispaniola and Jamaica have railways had any importance, and even there they have now been mostly abandoned or superseded by road transport.

In Jamaica the railway has survived in reasonable shape, and although the facilities are somewhat inadequate (there are wooden seats still and the stations are rather run-down) the Jamaican Railway Corporation runs regular services between Kingston and Montego Bay via Spanish Town, with a branch line to Port Antonio. The trains are diesel-driven (the changeover from steam to diesel took place in 1963) and fares are low. The 100-mile journey from Kingston to Montego Bay takes about four hours and a half. There are some 230 miles of track in all, with another 20 miles operated on behalf of Alcoa, the bauxite company. About 75 per cent of the revenue is from freight, but about $1\frac{1}{4}$ million passengers were carried in 1969. The railway makes a substantial loss and it is rather doubtful whether it can survive indefinitely, especially as car ownership continues to increase.

In Trinidad the railway system operated from 1876 to 1968 and linked Port of Spain with San Fernando: there were 109 miles of standard-gauge track. The railway lines were sold to Venezuela recently as scrap metal, while the remains of the rolling stock can be seen lying in a derelict siding outside the capital. There are some people who bemoan the loss of the railway and urge that it be revived as one solution to the growing problem of traffic congestion, but the cost would be high and the flexibility of road transport is such that a revival of rail transport seems unlikely.

The small islands never had a standard-gauge railway system, but a number of narrow-gauge railways are used mainly in connection with the sugar industry. In the

Bahamas there were small lumber railways on Grand Bahama and Inagua, and an interesting new proposal has been mooted in recent years for a monorail to be built linking the airport on Grand Bahama with Freeport. Perhaps this may signal the beginning of a new chapter in the story of railways in the West Indies.

7

How They Amuse Themselves

Music

Music, dancing and carnival are in the blood of the West Indians, and they will always be an indelible part of the way of life of the islanders.

In the 1930s the police in Trinidad banned the carrying of bamboo sticks (used for making music) in communal processions, and this led the local music-makers to experiment with old garbage tins. So evolved the steel drum, the only completely new musical instrument that has emerged in the world in recent times. The steel drums or 'pans' are becoming identified more and more with indigenous West Indian culture. They are used not only for calypsos but also for all kinds of classical music. There are some thirty to forty leading steel-drum bands in Trinidad and each one has its large group of supporters. Steel-drum contests have become a very popular feature of the annual carnival.

Other instruments used for making music in West Indian style include the guitar, and also the fiddle which is popular among the Irish people of Barbados where Irish jigs are still danced. Tambourines are widely used, often in religious ceremonies and in the wayside chapels. Wind instruments of various kinds are most popular with the East Indians in Trinidad.

Classical music was inevitably identified historically with the ruling classes and slave owners and has played a less

142

important part in the life of the ordinary people than music of folk origin. However, there is now increasing interest in it. The main problem is that because of the small audiences available in the islands it is very difficult to attract orchestras or performers of high calibre, while local musicians generally have to leave the West Indies if they want to make real progress in classical music. Thus the islands of the West Indies are starved of good classical music. It was a great step forward when the late Pablo Casals, the celebrated cellist, established the Casals Music Festival in Puerto Rico where he had lived for many years. This is held annually in May or June and attracts top performers. Puerto Rico has made great efforts to develop cultural life and has recently launched 'Operation Serenity', to succeed 'Operation Bootstrap', in an effort to encourage the arts. Already the new Puerto Rican Symphony Orchestra has been established, the first of its kind in the West Indies, and symphony concerts are held regularly, while live theatre and ballet are flourishing as well. In Trinidad too, efforts are being made to stimulate interest in music. It has the fine Queen's Concert Hall, but at present this is virtually unused so far as concerts are concerned. There are however an Indian National Orchestra and a Trinidad Music Festival. In 1970 the new Folk Company was established, under the patronage of Aubrey Adams, to experiment with new musical forms and to develop a greater appreciation of music of all forms and traditions in the island: Indian and Chinese as well as Negro and European. In Jamaica musical activities are very limited, although the School of Music in Kingston arranges concerts occasionally.

Calypso

Music has often been for the West Indian an outlet for bottled-up emotions: a vehicle of protest, at first against the system of slavery and later against the prevailing conditions of poverty and economic degradation. But not only protest. Music was also the spontaneous expression of the West

Indian's *joie de vivre*, the bubbling up of his innate sense of fun. Whether it was protest or simply pleasure, the West Indian's natural way of expressing his feelings was in a torrent of words set loosely to music. And so the calypso was born. The calypso is a folk-song composed originally on the spur of the moment and relating to some topical individual or incident, often critical of people in high positions, and in recent times using language that borders on the obscene. The two most famous calypsos are *Rum and Coca-Cola* and *Brown Skin Gal*.

Dancing

Music, song and dancing have always gone together in the Caribbean, and it is in the dance that the West Indian most naturally expresses himself. You can see how his toes start tapping the moment a band starts up. There are many different threads woven into the tapestry of music and dancing in the West Indies: the rituals of tribal Africa, Roman Catholicism and Hindu ceremonies, Protestant evangelicism, the protest against slavery, the jazz groups of New Orleans and of Harlem . . . they have all contributed to the rhythms and movements of Caribbean dances. In the interior of Martinique dances like the calenda, the *haute taille* and the *bel air* (which are almost purely African in origin) survive; in Trinidad the Hindus perform a ritual sabre dance to the music of tambourines; in Haiti one can witness in the Théâtre Verdure (a primitive shack, lit by candles, on the outskirts of Port au Prince) ancient spirit-possession dances derived from a weird mixture of Roman Catholic and voodoo influences; in Puerto Rico they dance the plena to the rhythm of the rumba. Both the plena and the merengue (the national dance of Haiti and the Dominican Republic) are derived from a mixture of Spanish and African influences. The European influence has survived in its purest form in Martinique where the girls still dance the mazurka and, as tradition demands, swoon into the arms of their partners at the conclusion of the dance. In Trinidad one finds the old pagan dance the shango, derived from ancient Yoruba rituals, together with the more modern 'jump up', bongo and limbo. In the Bahamas people go through the streets at festival times, especially on Boxing Day and at New Year, doing the junkanoo: this is a masked dance which can be traced back to Jamaica as early as 1801. It is in fact less a dance than a parade, a kind of miniature carnival; the people dress in crêpe-paper costumes and dance through the streets to the accompaniment of drums, whistles and cowbells, and in recent years floats have been added, especially in the big parades like those in Nassau. All in all, the West Indies has a rich tradition of dancing.

Carnival

Music, song and dance reach their climax in the annual carnival, a feature of all those islands which have a French or Spanish background, and above all in Trinidad, the 'Land of Carnival', where it has long been the great social event of the year. Carnival, or 'masquerade' as it used to be called, is an amalgam of religious ceremonies and folk music and dancing. At first it was considered to be a very 'low' form of social activity, suitable only for the working classes, and the obscenity of some of the calypsos confirmed the matrons of the Caribbean in this opinion. But more recently, a marked change in attitude has taken place. Like the steel drum, carnival has become respectable. The political leaders are in part responsible for this, as they have come to feel that carnival can be valuable in generating a more lively sense of West Indian identity, thus helping in the struggle for independence, and in building up a sense of national pride and West Indian consciousness. In 1956 the People's National Movement in Trinidad recognised carnival as a national cultural heritage to be promoted and encouraged as much as possible. Since then it has been well and truly 'nationalised', and Derek Walcott, the West Indian playwright, has dignified it with the title of 'the theatre of the streets'. Carnival has come to play an ever increasing role in the social life not only of Trinidad *par excellence* but also of other islands. In Haiti, *mardi gras,* as it is called there, takes place three days before Ash Wednesday—three days of tumultuous fun before the priest plants a fingertip of ash on the forehead of the faithful and 'the carnival is over'.

On most of the other islands the pattern is similar, but there are special features such as the burning of King Vaval in Martinique, as night falls on Ash Wednesday, to the accompaniment of moaning and groaning in the streets. At one time masks were commonly worn, as the old title 'masquerade' suggests, but these are seldom seen now, one reason being that in times past the wearing of masks was often used as an excuse for paying off old scores and carnival became too frequently an occasion for violence.

Festivals

Carnival is but one of the many festivals and parades which add an extra touch of colour to life in the West Indies. In Puerto Rico for instance there is a great number of feast days and festivals and everyone has his own patron saint whose day is duly honoured with colourful parades and festivities. Easter parades last a whole week, whilst the sugar-cane harvest also is heralded by special celebrations. Christmas is of course celebrated everywhere in the West Indies, and each island has its own traditions, such as the parang in Trinidad, ie the singing of local Christian songs. In many of the islands Discovery Day, the day when Christopher Columbus first discovered their island, is celebrated as a national holiday. Choosing beauty queens and carnival queens is one of the great social activities of the West Indians and this may explain why the region has had so many successes in the Miss World competitions.

Specifically religious festivals play an important part, particularly in those islands with a Roman Catholic tradition, and on Trinidad with its large Hindu and Moslem population. Corpus Christi Day is the occasion for sumptuous parades and the carrying of banners and religious objects through the streets. On All Saints Day candles are lit in the cemeteries, and on Christmas Day cribs are erected in prominent places such as the Botanical Gardens in Port of Spain, Trinidad. In Puerto Rico the eve of St John's Day is celebrated with all-night vigils and bonfires in honour of the saint after whom the capital of San Juan is named. In Trinidad the Moslems celebrate the festival of Hosein with parades of the colourful tadgeah (a beautifully executed bamboo model of a mosque decorated with tinsel, coloured paper and glass—it is thrown into the sea when the festival is over) and also the ritual of Eid-ul-Fitr, while the Hindus also have their festivals: one in honour of spring and that of Divali, the beautiful festival of lights.

SPORTS

Water sports

As one would expect from an island people, the West Indians enjoy all kinds of water sports, from scuba-diving to water-skiing, and these sports are extremely popular also with the visitors to the islands who often come primarily for the opportunity of enjoying the region's incomparable facilities.

Swimming is of course the leading water sport, and the beautiful beaches and reef-enclosed bays of many of the islands offer unequalled facilities. Puerto Rico alone has 600 miles of beach, while Antigua claims to have 365 beaches, a different one for each day of the year. Because of the clear water and the existence of subterranean coral-reefs, scuba-diving and snorkelling are growing rapidly in popularity, especially in the Bahamas, where the water is as clear at 50ft as it is at 5ft and where there is the added attraction of exploring the hundreds of old wrecks which litter the shallow waters of these islands (while the less venturesome content themselves with glass-bottomed boats). In the Virgin Islands one can take a skin-diving tour of the wreckage of the French luxury liner, the *Rhône,* which went down in a hurricane about 100 years ago. Jamaica's north shore, Tobago and Aruba are other locations famed for the sport. Although swimming and diving are normally reasonably safe, one has to take great care on the more exposed Atlantic shore of the islands in the Eastern Caribbean because of the powerful 'rip' currents and the pounding surf; swimming tragedies in these waters are unfortunately a common occurrence. Surf-riding is a popular sport, especially when the trade winds are blowing between December and April in such places as Maracas Bay, Trinidad, Eleuthera in the Bahamas and at Punta Higuero in Puerto Rico where the World Surfing Championships were held in 1968. Other good places for surfing are at the North Point Surf Resort, Barbados and Frigate Bay and Conareef Beach in St Kitts.

Yachting is another popular sport both with the local people and with visitors. The waters around New Providence in the Bahamas are considered to be among the finest in the world for sailing; but the Virgin Islands, with their thirty-six islands and many fine channels protected from the ocean swell by low-lying out-islands yet subject to the trade winds, and also the Grenadines, run them a close second. So popular has sailing become that many of the new tourist and residential developments now taking place in the Caribbean are centred around man-made marinas. The best weather for sailing is between November and June, avoiding the hurricane season in the late summer and autumn. Sudden squalls occur and beginners need to heed the advice of local experts, while another hazard is the danger of hidden reefs close inshore. The chartering of yachts has become a flourishing business and at least one such company increased its profits tenfold between 1969 and 1971. Motor-powered boats are also popular and are used widely for water-skiing and fishing. Barbados holds a water-skiing festival every February, and the sport is particularly popular in the calmer waters of the Bahamas and the Virgin Islands. The annual Bahamas '500' Powerboat Race in Nassau Harbour is considered to be the top boat-race in the world.

Fishing has always been an important activity in the West Indies, but fishing for sport is relatively new and has been given a great stimulus by the growth of tourism. The tourists go mostly for deep-sea fishing and special tournaments are held in such centres as Antigua, the Bahamas and the Virgin Islands. At one such event recently in the British Virgin Islands, a blue marlin weighing 225lb was displayed (Puerto Rico has the world record of 780½lb). Records are being broken every year in this sport as in most others. Most of the fishing takes place in the waters surrounding the islands. River fishing is rare because such rivers as there are in the islands are usually short and are either very shallow or raging torrents following a great downpour of rain—hardly ideal conditions for the sport.

Golf and tennis

As in so many other parts of the world, the West Indies in recent years has experienced an 'explosion' of interest in golfing as a sport. Again this has been due primarily to the swift growth of tourism, as golfing is an expensive sport, but the local people also are rapidly acquiring an interest in the game now that more and more courses are being built. Puerto Rico leads with a number of very fine championship-standard courses linked to the large hotels. For instance the Dorado Beach and Cerromar Beach hotels will shortly have between them four 18-hole golf-courses. Jamaica has nine 18-hole courses, the Bahamas eight and Barbados two. Many other islands have 9-hole courses. St Kitts is building an 18-hole course in connection with the Frigate Bay tourist complex.

Tennis is played throughout the Caribbean, often on hard courts because of the difficulty of keeping grass courts in good condition, although in the Windward Islands a Lawn Tennis Association has been formed recently and others exist elsewhere. Virtually all the hotels have their own tennis courts attached, and the game is particularly popular in the French islands.

Team sports

The leading team sport in those islands with a British background is cricket. Although the game was introduced only as recently as the 1850s it rapidly became very popular and today one sees it being played all over the British West Indies wherever a few boys can find an odd stretch of grass, a piece of palm frond for a bat and an old paraffin tin for a wicket. When the test matches are being played in the West Indies, everything else has to take second place—only carnival claims a greater importance as an event in the social calendar. Among the many famous West Indian cricketers are Lord Learie Constantine, who did so much to improve race relations during his latter years in Britain, George Hedley, Gary Sobers (who now plays mainly in England), Clyde Walcott and Frank Worrell.

In Puerto Rico and the Dominican Republic, and to a lesser extent in the Bahamas, the most popular team sport is baseball. The season lasts from October to March and games are played in the Hiram Bithorn stadium in San Juan and at stadiums in five other cities in Puerto Rico. The enthusiasm for the game in Puerto Rico exceeds even that in the USA. Baseball is also played in the Dominican Republic and in Aruba. The American influence reveals itself too in the popularity of softball and basketball in these islands.

Soccer is the main team sport in many of the islands, particularly in Haiti where there are games every night in the stadium in Port au Prince, drawing up to 25,000 people.

Soccer is also popular in the Dominican Republic, Trinidad (where it is called 'football') and Jamaica where it is played all the year round. Soccer is the principal sport also in the French islands, where the annual Easter Sunday game between Guadeloupe and Martinique is the classic sporting event of the year; and in the Netherlands Antilles.

Polo is a popular sport in some of the islands of the British West Indies, particularly Jamaica and Barbados, largely owing to the British troops who were stationed there in times gone by. When the Prince of Wales attended the Bahamas independence celebrations in 1973, the occasion was marked by a polo match in which the Prince took part.

Mainly spectator sports

Boxing is one of the most popular spectator sports in the West Indies, and it crosses all the linguistic and cultural boundaries. It is as popular in the drill halls of Trinidad or Barbados as it is in the huge Sixto Escobar Stadium in San Juan (named after Puerto Rico's bantam-weight boxing champion).

Horse-racing, like polo, was popular with the military in the past and it can claim to be the oldest sport in the West Indies. It has since become popular with the public at large. Barbados holds races three times a year at the Barbados Turf Club. Jamaica has a fine race-course at Caymanas Park, Kingston and the El Commandante race-course in San Juan, Puerto Rico is used three times a week throughout the year; it is one of the most beautiful in the world. Trinidad (Queen's Park) and Nassau (Hobby Horse Hall) also have race-courses, while St Vincent has one of the best known riding-stables in the Caribbean where the horses enjoy the luxury of air-conditioned surroundings. Other islands with courses include Tobago, Grenada, St Croix and the Dominican Republic (the Perla de las Antillas course in Santo Domingo).

Motor racing calls for very heavy capital expenditure both

for the track and for the cars and is therefore not found on many islands. However, there are tracks at Aruba and Nassau, and in Puerto Rico the Ramsey airbase is used for this purpose every July. Trinidad also uses an airfield for the sport pending the construction of a new Grand Prix circuit.

A curious survival from earlier times is the sport which has been banned in Britain since 1849 and which is illegal in most countries of the world except South Africa—cock-fighting. The sport, if it can be called that, is found mainly in Haiti where fights are held every Monday at the Coq d'or in the Exposition grounds; and one of the most important buildings in the new town of Duvalierville is the cockpit. Cock-fighting is found also in Puerto Rico, the Dominican Republic, the French islands and in St Martin. In Puerto Rico it is the most popular sport after baseball, and there are cockpits at Santurce near San Juan and in many other cities. The main interest lies in the betting, but it is curious that so many of the West Indians continue to indulge in a sport which most other countries consider cruel and degrading. The same applies to bull-fighting which continues to be popular in Puerto Rico.

Other sporting activities

Among the other sporting activities to be found in the West Indies are: athletics, particularly in Jamaica and Trinidad which have produced many well-known athletes; bowling, particularly in Puerto Rico where many new boleras have been built recently; hockey, especially in Trinidad; horse-riding, a popular activity in Puerto Rico where the Dorado Hilton stables include the famed Paso Fino horses bred from stallions and brood mares said to have been brought over by Columbus, and also in Barbados, Jamaica, Antigua and St Croix; mountain climbing, mainly in the Windward Islands such as St Lucia and Dominica, and in the Blue Mountains of Jamaica; stick fighting in Trinidad—half sport and half religious ceremony and wholly dangerous; and flying in light aircraft. The latter sport is popular in Jamaica (forty-eight airstrips); Puerto Rico (San Juan has an enterprising flying school where one can 'rent a plane'); in the Bahamas and in Aruba. In the Bahamas they hold an annual Flying Treasure Hunt for small private aeroplanes. Jamaica in 1970 arranged its first annual 'Fly-in'.

There must surely be no other region of the world, of comparable size, with a richer choice of sporting facilities, and even though many of these at present are enjoyed mainly by the tourists, the West Indians themselves are taking part increasingly and this trend will continue. It is not for nothing that the West Indies has earned the reputation of being the 'playground of the world'.

STAGE, SCREEN AND RADIO

Theatre

As one would expect, the commercial theatre scarcely exists in the Caribbean because of the problems of small scale Puerto Rico has the elegant Tapia Theatre in San Juan, but there is no resident company; however, it has its own professional ballet company (Ballets de San Juan) but this has to be subsidised heavily by the government. Jamaica has its National Dance Theatre and Trinidad had its Empire Theatre in Port of Spain before this was burned down in the 1940s. Theatre in the Caribbean either depends heavily on government patronage and is closely linked to State-organised festivals of culture and the like, or it is purely amateur, operating on a shoe-string in 'little theatres' or whatever building can be pressed into service. Trinidad and Tobago, with its Ministry of Education and Culture, has gone a long way in the direction of organising cultural activities on a State basis. In 1968 the New Little Carib Theatre was opened in Port of Spain, and at the laying of the foundation stone the prime minister, Dr Eric Williams, said: 'It is a landmark on

K

the long road which the West Indian people have been patiently travelling for several years, in an attempt to encourage locally the creative talent which would generally in the past be satisfied only by emigration.' Plays in the local dialect are staged here and draw high praise. Many experimental activities are arranged in an attempt to synthesise the many cultures that make up the Trinidadians.

Other Caribbean islands have their Little Theatres, or amateur theatrical groups. Antigua has had a community theatre group for the last twenty years and similar groups exist in Jamaica, Puerto Rico, St Kitts and St Lucia among others. In the French islands, however, there is a greater dependence upon metropolitan France for entertainment and less enthusiasm for indigenous cultural activities.

Cinema

The cinema is very popular throughout the West Indies and long queues can be seen frequently, especially in those islands where television has not yet arrived. New cinemas are being built on many of the islands. Even tiny Anguilla has now acquired a large new cinema at Farrington which is the largest building on the island. In the larger islands drive-in cinemas are popular. The films shown are mainly American (even in Puerto Rico where they are subtitled in Spanish) and the cinema has been a powerful agent for the spreading of American ideas and idioms throughout the Caribbean. British and French films also are shown and occasionally Spanish-language ones (usually from Mexico). So far the film-making industry in the West Indies has hardly got off the ground, but there are signs of an indigenous industry's being established soon. Studio facilities have been built at Buckingham County in Grand Bahama, and in Trinidad, where two full-length films were produced in 1971. Several films have been made on location in Jamaica and there is now a film studio at Cinema City, Montego Bay. Locally made newsreels and commercials are shown in Puerto Rico.

Radio and television

Radio has for many years played an important part in Caribbean life and nearly every family owns a wireless or a transistor radio. In Barbados a recent survey showed that 44 per cent of the people owned a wireless, ie more than one per family. In Trinidad 78 per cent of the population is estimated to listen to the radio every day. The Netherlands Antilles has no less than twelve radio stations, the Dominican Republic has seventy, Haiti seventeen and Puerto Rico fifteen, two of which broadcast programmes in English.

Many of the radio stations are run on a commercial basis and the advertising has a decidedly American flavour. However, there are also government-run stations which are either wholly subsidised or, like the Jamaican Broadcasting Corporation ('The Voice of Jamaica'), are empowered to sell time commercially provided they broadcast government-sponsored items on request. In the French Antilles all the stations are run by the government.

There has been some local co-operation for a number of years, particularly in the Windward Islands where the Windward Islands Broadcasting Service (non-commercial) transmits programmes covering the four islands as a group. In recent years the degree of co-ordination has increased greatly with the establishment in 1970 of the Caribbean Broadcasting Union (CBU), the first organisation of its kind in the world. This arranges for joint news coverage of all the thirteen member countries evey day, and also musical and current affairs programmes of regional interest. The CBU has no money of its own and the basic problem is that the member stations have to rely mainly on their advertising revenue and cannot devote much time or money to programmes which yield no income. However, the CBU has got off to a good start and is serving a vital need.

Television is still relatively new in most of the islands, having arrived in the larger islands around the early 1960s, but it is making rapid headway. All the larger islands now have their own television studios. In Barbados in 1972 13 per cent of the people owned television sets, and in Jamaica it is estimated that 16 per cent of the people watch television every day. The Dominican Republic in 1970 had 100,000 television receivers for over 4 million people. Puerto Rico has six television stations and the programmes are strongly American in character. Throughout the Caribbean indeed television has been a leading Americanising influence as many of the programmes shown are 'canned' from the USA. The people of Grand Bahama are able to receive television direct from Florida thanks to the community antennae cable service. As with radio, many of the television stations depend in whole or in part on advertising for their revenue, although some governments have made stipulations regarding the maximum time that can be allocated to advertising: in Trinidad for instance it is 12·5 per cent. The mountainous nature of some of the islands is a real handicap in ensuring whole-island coverage, while the fact that not all rural areas have as yet been electrified is another obstacle. Another problem in getting television to the rural areas is that the potential income from advertising in these areas is so small that it does not cover the cost of additional transmitters. To overcome the problem of too high a proportion of programmes being 'canned' or in the form of old films, some governments stipulate a minimum of live transmissions per day. In Barbados for instance this is set at one hour. Educational programmes are playing an increasing role in school curricula, particularly in view of the continuing scarcity of teachers. As to colour television, this is still in its infancy, but it is now being introduced in the larger islands.

LITERATURE, PRESS, PAINTING AND SCULPTURE

West Indian literature can be said to have begun in the 1920s with the writings of Claude McKay, but its first real flowering came in the 1950s with writers like V. S. Naipaul,

George Lamming and Samuel Selvon, all of whom published successful novels at this time. However, the characters in their books seemed to want to subdue their West Indian backgrounds and to become 'British' as quickly and as completely as possible. One of them, Pandit G. Ramsumair in Naipaul's *The Mystic Masseur* (1957) translated himself on emigrating to London to G. Ramsay Muir Esq MBE! However, by the 1960s a remarkable change had taken place. West Indian writers seemed to have rediscovered their pride in being West Indian. V. S. Naipaul himself led the way with his very successful *A Home for Mr Biswas* (1961), probably the first West Indian novel of world significance, and Derek Walcott's poetry gave fresh lustre to West Indian writing. In keeping with this new spirit and the stimulus of freshly acquired independence during the early 1960s, there was a wave of new interest in West Indian dialect plays and novels and a new pride in everything genuinely West Indian. As a character in Selvon's story, *The Calypsonian*, says: 'They does think calypso is no song at all and that what is song is numbers like "I've got you under my skin", what real American composers write.' Now writers were beginning to question conventional attitudes. In Haiti, writers like Jean Price-Mars were trying to elevate Negro pride in their African heritage, and in the French Antilles Senghor, with his 'Negritude' movement was busy fostering a new interest in the history and development of Negro culture. In the British West Indies, however, the writers adopted a less militant stand: they were more anxious to probe deeper into the nature of West Indian life and society—to try to understand it better. Dr Eric Williams, Prime Minister of Trinidad, for instance made his own contribution to this process in his brilliant *From Columbus to Castro, the History of the Caribbean, 1492–1969*. One has the feeling that literature in the West Indies stands at the threshold of a mini-renaissance, as more and more writers respond to the stimulus of a people newly literate, newly independent, newly conscious of the richness and vitality of their society, and newly able to read and enjoy books.

To the average West Indian at present, reading matter means primarily the newspapers, and these are devoured hungrily from cover to cover, often being passed on from person to person. Even Dominica, with a population of about 70,000, has four newspapers. A recent survey in Barbados showed that 60 per cent of families regularly read a newspaper or magazine. Only in Haiti, where illiteracy is still frighteningly high, are newspapers still the preserve of the *élite* 7,000 who are estimated to constitute the readership of the six newspapers. In the French Antilles local newspapers are non-existent, not because the people cannot read but because they rely wholly on the papers brought over from France. As Naipaul has remarked rather scathingly: 'The newspapers come from Paris with the milk.' But elsewhere the press is a key element in West Indian life and thought. Trinidad and the Bahamas have two daily newspapers; Jamaica has only one, but a second, the *Gleaner* was launched in 1973, the first new daily since 1938.

Often the standard of political reporting in the newspapers is very low and they resort to considerable personal abuse of the worst kind, with ceaseless sniping on the part of the opposition party papers at whatever the government does, good or bad. Some of the islands, notably St Kitts and Antigua, have introduced legislation recently in an attempt to prohibit publications considered 'scurrilous, seditious and blasphemous, and that so distort information as to be likely to deceive the public in matters of public interest'. There have been cries of protest at what is considered to be an attack on the freedom of the press, but freedom involves responsibility and some of the opposition newspapers have undoubtedly abused the freedom they have enjoyed. Politics apart, the papers are full of items of local news interest and they successfully combine the functions of a national daily and a local weekly.

Painting and sculpture come naturally to the West Indians, encouraged perhaps by their natural environment of blue skies, splendid seascapes and sharply defined colours. It is no accident that West Indian painting is characterised by the strong use of colour and vivid imagery. The 'primitives' of Haiti, a curious blend of African and Christian symbolism and a Van Gogh-like passion for bright colours (there are some large examples placed strategically in the passenger terminal at the harbour of Port au Prince), have achieved world-wide fame. The West Indians start experimenting with colours at an early age and children's exhibitions are frequently held. Sculpture is also popular and Edna Manley, one of Jamaica's leading sculptresses, has done much to stimulate renewed interest in Negro sculpture. Another Negro sculptor, Alvin Marriott, made the statue of Sir Alexander Bustamente in Victoria Square, Kingston, Jamaica. Several island governments are taking positive steps to encourage and promote the arts. Trinidad for example is to build a new cultural centre on the historic Princess Building site in Port of Spain which will include a creative arts centre (neither Trinidad nor Jamaica has proper art galleries at present) a visual arts hall, an Afro-Asian museum and a national archives building. Puerto Rico also has a government-sponsored programme to encourage the arts which are already well established in the island. The artists' quarter of Old San Juan is the New World's Montmartre. In addition to the San Juan Museum of Art there is a magnificent new Museum of Art at Ponce, which has been referred to sometimes as the Parthenon of the Caribbean. The silk-screen printing in Puerto Rico has achieved wide renown, as have the *santos*, or small religious objects, carved from hardwood.

As to the smaller islands, they have their own small arts festivals, like those of Antigua and St Kitts. In Martinique the Caribbean Art Centre at Fort de France has some highly original wall hangings, as well as paintings, sculpture and craftwork of a high standard. A recent conference of Caribbean heads of government decided that a Caribbean Festival of Creative Arts should be held in a different country every three years. Admirable though all these government-sponsored initiatives are, it is to be hoped that the governments will not become over-involved in the arts, since in the long run this may not create a climate in which the arts can flourish most readily. One senses for instance distinct dangers in the recent decision of the Trinidad Government consciously to associate all trade and tourism promotion endeavours with efforts to popularise West Indian art and culture. West Indian art is still a young and tender plant and it may need some discreet fertilising and a receptive soil, but it has plenty of hybrid vigour of its own, and given adequate air and light and not too much interference, it should grow as luxuriantly as most other plants seem to do in the Caribbean.

8

Hints for Visitors

VISITORS are welcome throughout the Caribbean, and during the main tourist season, mid-December to mid-April, the islands are crowded with tourists. It is very rare that there is any hostility to foreigners, and there is little colour consciousness. A particularly warm welcome awaits the visitor who is genuinely interested in how the people live and work as well as wanting to enjoy the region's unrivalled sporting and other amenities. Increasingly, arrangements are being made to show visitors round the sugar or citrus plantations, rum or cigar factories and sites of special historical interest.

Most visitors to the Caribbean arrive by air, and it is worth remembering that some air fares, if ordered and paid for three months in advance, can be bought very economically. All visitors from Britain require a valid international certificate of vaccination against smallpox. A British driving licence is acceptable everywhere. Visas are not normally required, but both Puerto Rico and the American Virgin Islands are part of the USA and visitors to these islands will need visas. Visas may be needed also for Haiti—it is as well to check. If you are visiting the British Virgin Islands, remember that a visa will be necessary if you want to cross over to the American Virgin Islands.

The American dollar is the main currency in both the American Virgin Islands and the British Virgin Islands. The currency situation can be confusing, because the Eastern Caribbean dollar (together with the Trinidad and Tobago dollar) has a different value from the Jamaican or Bahamian

161

dollar and only the latter has a 1:1 ratio with the American dollar. It is wise to obtain up-to-date exchange rates before leaving, and to change traveller's cheques in banks if possible rather than in hotels, as the rate of exchange is likely to be more favourable.

When swimming, remember that the currents can be powerful, especially on the Atlantic coast. If caught in a 'rip' current flowing strongly out to sea, do not try to fight it but instead swim parallel with the shore and you should then soon get out of the current. Beware of the sharp coral-reefs and also of sea-urchin prickles which can be very painful. It is best to wear soft shoes when exploring the reefs. On the Atlantic shores watch out for stinging jelly-fish and Portuguese men-of-war.

Photographers should keep their films in an air-conditioned room or refrigerator: film can be badly damaged by heat, as the author has discovered to his cost. A lens hood will be useful as a protection against strong reflection of light.

Humidity can be high at times in the West Indies, particularly in Trinidad and in the Netherlands Antilles. Remember also that it can rain heavily on some of the islands, so a light plastic raincoat is useful. On the other hand bear in mind that, even if the sky is grey, the sun can still burn between noon and 3 pm and a siesta during this period is not a bad idea.

Learn to adopt the more relaxed way of life of the West Indians. There is no need to rush. After all, this is not a New York subway or the London Underground.

Bibliography

THE MOST up-to-date sources for recent events in the West Indies are the monthly *West Indian Chronicle* and the quarterly *West Indian Review*. The *Yearbook of the Caribbean* is also very valuable, particularly for business people; tourists too may find its information on hotels useful, although it may be rather out of date, as the yearbook takes a long time to assemble.

More specialised journals which often have useful information are *Caribbean Studies*, *The Farmer*, *International Tourism Quarterly*, *Tropical Doctor* and the *Financial Times* supplements on the Caribbean.

Recently published books of particular interest are:

Barratt, P. J. H. *Grand Bahama* (David & Charles, 1972)

Beckford, G. L. *Persistent Poverty* (New York: OUP, 1972)

Clarke, Edith. *My Mother Who Fathered Me* (George Allen & Unwin, 2nd ed 1966)

Cracknell, B. E. *Dominica* (David & Charles, 1973)

Crampsey, R. A. *Puerto Rico* (David & Charles, 1973)

Hamshere, C. *The British in the Caribbean* (Weidenfeld & Nicolson, 1972)

Harknett, T. *The Caribbean* (New English Library, 1972)

Hunte, G. *The West Indian Islands* (Batsford, 1972)

Leyburn, J. G. *Haitian People* (Yale University Press, rev ed 1966)

Lynch, L. *The Barbados Book* (Andre Deutsch, 2nd ed 1972)

Mitchell, Sir Harold. *Caribbean Patterns* (Chambers, 1972)

Acknowledgements

WITH a book of this kind one has to seek help from so many people that it is impossible to acknowledge them all. However, I would like to single out the following who were specially helpful.

In Barbados, the late Mr G. Bynoe of the Barbados Sugar Producers Association, and Mr Bill Bell, lately Head of the British Development Division, and his colleague Mr David Tipping; in Trinidad, Dr T. H. Henderson and Professor D. Edwards of the University of the West Indies; in St Lucia, Mr Andrew Tench; in Dominica, Mr C. Sorhaindo, until recently Financial Secretary, Mr G. Robinson and Mr S. Pringle of the Ministry of Agriculture, and Mrs Cynthia Baker of the University of Swansea; in Jamaica, Mr W. V. Elliott of the All Islands Cane Farmers Association, and Mr David Lord of the Jamaica Banana Marketing Board. In London I received invaluable help from Miss Wendy Jolly of the East Caribbean Tourist Office, Mr Jack Spector of Winban who is a great authority on bananas, Mr Shillingford of the Eastern Caribbean Governments Commission, and from the librarians of the West India Committee and the Overseas Development Ministry.

Finally, I owe a great debt of gratitude to my wife Sylvia for bearing so patiently with my long absences in the West Indies —and with those equally long absences pounding a typewriter in the room next door.

Index

165